TELLING TALES OUT OF SCHOOL

A Memoir
By
Mary E.
Furlong

Copyright © 2021, Mary E. Furlong

All illustrations have been provided by the author.

Book design by Mike Miller.
ISBN: 9798762487542

In Memory of Barbara Orr (1933-2020)

****

****

It only takes me two weeks to whip a class out of shape.
(Recalled from the Wit and Wisdom of Barbara Orr)

Introduction

To pack thirty-five years of teaching into a little more than 100 pages is a challenging task, all the more so because recollection leads to a reconsideration of the meaning of what happened. Which is to say, as many writers have before me, that I sometimes don't know what I mean until I've said it. And then, of course, I have to say it again just to be sure I've been clear.

Here are some things I hope I've made clear:

- There is nothing more challenging than to spend one's days with young children.
- There is nothing more rewarding than to spend one's days with young children.
- Little kids know more about the world of grown-ups than we think they do.
- We grown-ups know less about the world of little kids than we think we do.
- I could go on and on.
- You wish I wouldn't go on and on, but just get on with the book. So here goes:

It seems that I was destined to be a teacher. My mother, my aunt, and several of my cousins were teachers, so it was assumed that I would be one, too. Besides, there were very few career options for women when I was making choices. Teacher, nurse, secretary – that was about it. I was scared to even think about nursing. I was much too disorganized to be a secretary. And teaching required a college education, including lots of the liberal arts. This was true no matter what or whom you were going to teach.

I desperately wanted to study history and literature and all the other liberal arts stuff. So, I went to New York State Teachers College at Buffalo, enjoyed all the liberal arts stuff, and became a teacher.

Along the way, there was a lot of controversy about what kind of teacher I would become. Here's the gist of it:

- A middle-grade teacher like her, my mother imagined.
- An English teacher, of course, thought my college English teacher.
- A first-grade teacher, stated Geraldine J. Mann, elementary supervisor for the Niagara Falls public schools. Miss Mann didn't say so directly, but I knew – and she knew I knew – that she was saving the intermediate grades for the men, who were beginning to show an interest in teaching young children but-weren't ready to go so far as to teach the very youngest of them.
- Maybe a librarian instead, I offered tenuously. (I had an after-school dream job at the La Salle branch of the Niagara Falls public library when I was in high school. With Mrs. Fred Campbell in charge, that library was the social hub of the La Salle end of town – a far cry from the hush-hush atmosphere of most libraries. Common sense (i.e., my mother) told me that the idea of becoming a Mrs. Campbell-type librarian was a daydream, not a realistic goal. Nevertheless, I gave it some serious thought. And then, settled on first grade for all the reasons Miss Mann failed to articulate.

I know. I know. As women, she and I should both have protested such assumptions of privilege on the part of the guys! But I confess, we didn't give it much thought back then. At least, *I* didn't. The term 'male chauvinist' hadn't been invented yet and wouldn't be for a decade or more to come.

Anyway, I landed in the primary grades. And although the assignment didn't fit me like a glove, the primary grades proved to be more interesting, more challenging, and more rewarding than anything I could have imagined. As I wrote the following pages, I developed a greater appreciation of the thirty-five years I spent there. Time and again, incident after incident, story after story, I realized that little kids are wiser, funnier, more philosophical than I ever knew, so much so that I feared readers would think I was attempting fiction. "How old were these children?" some people asked, suspecting, it seemed, that I had created characters, not simply remembered them. It just goes to show how wise and insightful children can be. The fact is, you just can't make this stuff up.

The tales that I tell in this book are presented in random order, random being a hallmark of my approach to things. My original plan was to have all the first-grade stories come first, followed by the second-grade stories, but I strayed from this logical approach now and then. Sometimes, it's hard to tell the difference between the two age levels. Some first-graders are quite sophisticated and savvy; some second-graders cling to babyish ways.

While the incidents described in this book are true as I remember them, it should be noted that almost all names and some details have been changed to protect the privacy of the people involved. In some instances, separate events have been combined into one to avoid redundancy. (If both the given name and the surname are provided, as in the cases of some school administrators and public figures, the actual name has been used. I think these occurrences are clear from the various contexts.)

Childhood is measured out by
sounds and smells and sight
before the dark hour of reason settles in.

~Sir John Betjeman,
English poet, writer, and broadcaster

THE TALES - (and some poems)

DINO	2
BEFORE IT'S TOO LATE	7
BUSTER AND THE GIRLS	8
AND THE WINNER IS …	16
RIDDLE ME THIS	24
LAZARUS	26
THE MORAL OF THE STORY	34
LESLIE QUICK	40
A MODEST PROPOSAL	46
FRIDAY AFTERNOON	50
A FAIRY TALE BEGINNING	52
DEAR BIG BIRD	58
SWAK	64
BRAVE LITTLE GIRL	66
THE IMPORTANCE OF BEING EARNEST	72
A NEW DEAL	78
A SONG, A DANCE, AND A TRIBUTE	84
INCIDENT AT SUGAR HILL	92
YEAH, MANN!!!	98
ORANGE BALLOONS AND OTHER NECESSITIES	104
ACKNOWLEDGMENTS	111
ABOUT THE AUTHOR	112

DINO

    Once upon a time, a first-grade class at the Beech Avenue School in Niagara Falls, New York, decided to make a giraffe from papier-mâché and a sawhorse. No one knew why they wanted to do this. It just seemed like a good idea at the time.

When the giraffe was finished, he was a handsome creature indeed. Everyone in the school suggested names for him – clever names, like Stretch, Spot, Big Guy. Out of dozens of proposals, the kids chose the name Dino. No one knew why they preferred the name Dino. It just seemed like a good idea at the time.

Dino was so popular with all the kids and adults in the school that he was given a place of honor in the front hall, near the principal's office. He stood right inside the front door, where he was the first thing people saw when they came in.

Visitors to the school stopped to admire Dino. "He is beautiful," they all agreed. "But why did you put a giraffe in the front hall?"

No one knew what to tell them, except that it had seemed like a good idea at the time. And it still seemed like a good idea. So there he was.

One day, as the principal sat in his office with the door open, a little girl came skipping down the hall. When she came to Dino, she stopped, put her arms around his neck, and kissed him on the nose. Then off she skipped on her way

Now the principal thought he knew the reason for Dino. And so did I. And so did everyone. Dino was a symbol of in-betweenness – a stalwart lookout, craning his neck to see into the future, and a touchstone for all the childish things that kids are reluctant to put aside even as, with a skip and a jump, they approach the age of reason and logic.

It's a kind of Rubicon, that small space we call early childhood. Most people, once they have crossed it, can't really recall what they have left behind. Can't imagine that there was a time when two plus two didn't necessarily add up to four, even if you had been taught to say that it did. Can't recall how objects appeared to change their shapes and sizes to fit the circumstances: "I'm making a map of the world in the shape of a shoe," a bright little first-grader once told me. It would have been no use to inform him that we can't reshape the world no matter how much we might want to. He probably wouldn't have argued about it, but a part of him would have gone right on creating his map according to whatever concepts of maps and worlds his own experience had given him.

Experience is the operative word here. It has become a cliché to say that experience is the best teacher. But it's true; in fact, experience is the only teacher. Other people may guide, encourage, reinforce. But they can't offer a substitute for actually moving through space, touching and manipulating things, and talking, talking, talking about it all.

Someday, given time and opportunities to explore, that little map maker will have an aha moment about maps, the world, and his own capacity to influence them. At least, he will unless some impatient adult robs him of his moment by giving him information instead of experience. Even the most privileged of American kids, kids that are far from wanting in other respects, are often deprived of such moments

Here, right in the middle of darling Dino's story, are some statistics for you to chew on: Among five affluent nations measured for reading skills in their general populations, the United States and the United Kingdom have the highest incidence of illiteracy; Russia and Germany have more moderate levels of illiteracy. Denmark has almost no illiteracy problem at all.

Approaches to education in these five nations are as follows: The U. S. and the U.K. begin formal reading instruction at the age of four or five, sometimes even earlier. Russia and Germany start at five or six. Denmark delays formal reading instruction until the age of seven.

If you are into statistics, many others support the Denmark approach. You can look them up. Otherwise, back to Dino. The secret of his charm was that he was really good at nothing. Indeed, good *for* nothing. Just completely himself. He had no other reason for being except to be Dino. How reassuring is that for a little kid who is still trying on personas for size!

When school ended for the summer, Dino went on to claim a place in the window of a local insurance agency managed by one of the kids' Dads. The arrangement seemed like a good idea at the time. But the sun shining through the plate glass window began to fade his painted spots, so he moved on to a new home in the kindergarten teacher, Lettie Andre's backyard. There, he stood under an arbor, playing the role of not-a-flamingo until even the mild summer weather took its toll. His painted spots faded. His long neck sagged. *Sic Semper Camelopardalis* is fancy language for "so passes whatever species of giraffe Dino belonged to."

Alas, poor Dino. He finally succumbed to irredeemable shabbiness, for even a charmed life comes to an end. But during the short time he managed to remain intact, Dino represented the nowness of life, wherein the future shines with a brilliance that causes us to forget that the past had a radiance of its own. Over and over again, he proved that there are more things in heaven and on earth than are dreamed of in our grown-up philosophy. (That's a riff on "Hamlet," which just goes to show that, contrary to popular opinion, any number of us primary grade teachers read.)

In a way, Dino represents the essence of this book. He belongs to the contingent of characters and ideas that hold a special place in our imaginations – the ones that you have to adopt as your own when you are a child - Santa Claus, the Easter Bunny, etc., – for it will be too late once you are seven or so, once you become aware that there really is such a thing as acting your age. Thus, the title of the following ode to Dino.

BEFORE IT'S TOO LATE

And so, a toast to Dino, the keeper of the gate
Between the world of little kids and that of guys of eight.
That old world looks familiar to us who now reside
Beyond the time of childish things, but, oh, the gap is wide.
It's wider than we realize; rank foreigners are we,
Looking with our grown-up eyes at where home used to be.
And kids on their own journey to grown-upness often find
Themselves still longing, for the things they'll leave behind
Like faith in make-believe giraffes and creatures such as he
Whose whole excuse for being is quite simply just to be.

BUSTER AND THE GIRLS

Just so you know, there is no moral to this story. No epiphany. No lesson learned. No philosophical takeaway to change your perspective forever. If that's what you're looking for, turn the page. Because this ain't it, Kid.

Here's what it is: It's an episode, an incident, a happening that just happened to happen, as Dr. Seuss once said. It made me laugh at the time. And I still laugh whenever I think about it. As a memory, it's kind of in the category of seeing the musical "Cats" for the first time. It's delightful and fun, and you keep thinking it must mean something, but it doesn't. At least, I don't think it does. But I could be wrong. If I ever run into one of the little girls who participated, I'll ask.

That's right. Little girls. An all-girl first-grade class. No, I wasn't teaching in a convent school nor in Miss Simpson's Academy for Young Ladies. It was a public school, the classes segregated along gender lines as an experiment. My girls were leftovers in a way. The dregs. as it were, of a program designed for boys. The first-grade boys, as you may have guessed, formed an all-boy class taught by a male teacher, who, due to his inherent maleness, might prove to be a better role model than someone like me. It was an experiment, and so far, it was a huge success. As you may know, each and every educational experiment is, by definition, a huge success. Doomed to success, as someone once facetiously remarked. And thereafter, to peter out for one reason or another. Just one more example of education-related *plus ça change*.

My girls weren't in on the experiment, being, as I say, just the demographic leftovers, whose everyday successes went unnoticed – except by me. In the absence of boys, I had seen a subtle difference in the girls in this class. They were marginally more aggressive than girls I had taught in the past. More willing to try new things, unhampered by boys whose tendency was to push their way to the front of any line, to grab what they wanted to play with or use, to pester and tease in both obvious and subtle ways until the girls gave up and let them have what they wanted.

All of this is not to say that girls are the good guys and the boys are the outlaws. Girls have their own methods of jamming the wheels of progress. Gossiping, for instance. And creating social hierarchies. But this class seemed to have taken advantage of their all-girl status to break the mold and invent a new way of getting along together. As I say, it was a subtle thing – an attitude that I really couldn't put my finger on. In fact, I might never have done so if it hadn't been for some cutting-edge commercial teaching materials that came along in the nick of time.

According to their publishers, all new teaching materials are cutting-edge whether or not they're employed in one of those doomed experiments. It just goes without saying. Which is probably why Phil, this particular publishing company's sales rep, didn't mention the fact. He simply introduced us faculty members to his partner, Joan, "our company's top-notch language arts specialist." Did I think, Phil wondered, that my class might like to work with Joan? That way, some of us teachers could get an idea of how the new teaching materials would change our professional lives forever. Again, he didn't actually make this promise in so many words. Like the doom thing I just mentioned, it was implied.

I agreed to the top-notch specialist's demo. Why not? Thus, later that day, Phil and I and Mike, the first-grade boys' teacher, sat at the back of my classroom while Joan took over in top-notch fashion. She invited the girls to sit in a nice circle on the floor, just as they did for storybook time. She told them her full name and suggested that they call her Miss Joan. But that they should remember to raise their hands and wait for her to call on them before they did so. She raised her own hand to about ear-height to show them how it was done. One of the girls giggled – a portent of hilarity to come. But Miss Joan didn't see trouble coming. And, to be perfectly truthful, neither did I.

Rules established, Miss Joan moved on to the big reveal: Pictures. Ordinary black and white photos of ordinary little kids doing seemingly ordinary things in ordinary settings. They differed from other pictures in that they were big – blowups of ordinary size photos that you might find in an ordinary reading book. This, I surmised, was the cutting-edge factor that had been implied but never actually mentioned.

I could see the girls exchanging puzzled looks. This was baby stuff. What did it all mean? What were they supposed to say?

Miss Joan selected a picture. "Who can tell us what's happening here?" she asked, raising her own hand once again.

"That girl is bumping into that boy," said one of the girls – Susan – in a wondering tone. I understood her confusion. In her experience, boys did the bumping. Girls were always the bumpees.

Miss Joan nodded to show that she was listening. She waved her raised hand as a reminder of the correct protocol.

Susan ignored the waving hand. "Like this," she continued. And she hauled off and punched Laurie, the little girl sitting next to her. "Bump," she said by way of explanation.

No hard feelings apparently, for Laurie simply gave back as good as she got. "Yeah! Bump. Like this," she echoed. And the two of them dissolved into laughter.

"Don't be embarrassed," whispered Phil, who was seated behind me. "Joan's great. She can handle it."

"Well, then," said intrepid Miss Joan, handling it as promised. "What would you say to the little boy who got bumped?"

The answer came so quickly you'd have thought it was rehearsed: "Sorry about that, Buster."

Oh, that was a good one. Worthy of repetition. A chorus of 'sorry-about-that-Busters' ensued, the B sound more explosive with each rendering. One of my shyest ones, Mandy, rose to her knees and waved an imaginary baton as the phrase rang out with variations: "Sorry about that, Buster." "So-o-o sorry about that, Buster." "Really, really sorry, Buster."

Phil put his hand on my shoulder lest I interfere with Miss Joan's handling of things. No fear. I was too astounded to react. Who were these little monsters anyway? And who was Buster? And why was his name pronounced so explosively, especially the B sound? It began with lips pressed together in a prolonged Mmmm. Then, pow – they parted with a loud popgun sound that morphed into the requisite BUH for Buster, which was frequently followed by a loud, vulgar snort.

Between 'Busters,' the girls laughed. They threw their arms around each other, rocked back and forth, and laughed and laughed and laughed. Miss Joan, of course, did not laugh. Neither did she bolt and run. I have to give her credit for that. She stuck it out, raising her hand from time to time, but otherwise acting remarkably uninvolved.

"Don't be embarrassed," whispered Phil. "Nothing to be embarrassed about."

I nodded to show I understood. And then, to my amazement, I, too, began to laugh. Not out loud. That would be beyond rude, and the girls would be sure to notice. I laughed silently. I laughed until my sides hurt. Couldn't stop. Didn't even want to stop.

"Don't be …, "began Phil. And then, as he caught sight of my face, his own turned to stone. "It wouldn't hurt you to be a little bit embarrassed," he snarled.

I tried. I really, really tried to be a little bit embarrassed. But I couldn't do it. Mike stared at me in dismay, biting his lips so as not to be afflicted with whatever had possessed me. He glanced at his watch, apparently to check on his boys' gym time. It must be almost time to pick them up. I'm pretty sure he hoped so.

One good thing about first grade is that nothing lasts very long. The whole sorry episode happened in the space of about ten minutes. Then, the clock clicked loudly as schoolroom clocks always used to do. "Time for lunch," one of the girls said, and the laughter stopped cold. A harried Miss Joan began to pack her big pictures into their big box. I made my way forward to take charge of my class. Phil and Mike followed, Phil loyally moving to his partner's side.

"It was fine," I said, sincere and apologetic. "You got them to respond. I was afraid you wouldn't get a word out of them."

"Shut up," said the top-notch language-arts expert.

"Good-by, Miss Joan," said the kids, their sweet selves once again. "Thank you, Miss Joan." "Come again, Miss Joan."

Oh, butter wouldn't have melted in their mouths. Like honor students from Miss Simpson's Academy, for Young Ladies, they lined up at the door.

Joan didn't tell *them* to shut up. She didn't speak to them at all. And they, for their part, didn't notice that she didn't speak to them. It was pretty funny, her glowering, them not noticing. But I didn't laugh this time. No siree.

I guess I should have scolded the girls as we walked down the hall to the lunchroom. I should have reminded them that Miss Joan was a nice person who had been kind to them. I should have explained that she couldn't help it about the silly pictures. I should have told them I was ashamed of their behavior.

But I didn't. For one thing, my own behavior was nothing to brag about. And besides, to say I was ashamed of them would have been a lie. I liked the way they had refused to be belittled, the way they had made lemonade out of lemons, the way they had banded together in little girl solidarity.

I can't say I was proud of them. But I had a similarly good feeling – a subtle connection with them that I hadn't experienced before. As a result of their questionable behavior – *our* questionable behavior – we had what the French call 'rapport.' We were simpatico, my little girls and I. We were a team.

Of course, it was just a feeling. As I've said, there's really no deep meaning here. Something happened, and we laughed about it. When you come down to it, that's the sum total of the entire event.

Nevertheless, I felt there should be some accompaniment to our impromptu parade down the hallway -- the cocky strut that replaced our usual meandering amble. A ruffle of drums would be good. Or a fanfare. Or an anthem that we could all sing together – something perky like that Helen Reddy number: *I am woman; hear me roar.*

What? You don't get it? You think I'm unprofessional, disrespectful, even rude? You say that I'm lacking in judgment? That I have an attitude problem? Well, sorry about that, Buster.

AND THE WINNER IS ...

There's a lot of life going on in an elementary school hallway. It's a place for exploration, for kids to get to know teachers other than their own, for a little downtime before the school day begins, for checking out neighboring showcases and bulletin boards, for showing off show-and-tell items as a sort of preview to the real show-and-tell event. Sometimes, a Mom or two gets in on the act, stopping by to have a word about this or that that can't wait for parent conference day. (On one such occasion, a sweet little kindergartner introduced me to his mother, saying, "She never was my teacher, just my friend.")

We were all just friends during that few minutes before classes began. The hallway was like a giant office water cooler – a place to exchange gossip, tell jokes, admire each other's new sneakers. Little girls flirted shamelessly with the handsome third-grade teacher down the hall: *Don't look at me, Mr. C. I'm a complete mess this morning.* Kids complained that there was no safe place to put their snacks so they wouldn't get stolen before lunchtime. (We had a generic name for the light-fingered Louie of any given moment – the Frito Bandito). Safe in our own little corner of the world, we could hear mad-with-power members of the school safety patrol, stationed at the building's entrances, barking orders: *"Walk in the hall. No running. I said, WALK"* (One little girl thought the creature under the bridge in the three billy goats story was a big mean old patrol, an understandable confusion given the nature of these young tyrants.)

Yes, the hallway was a beehive of activity in the morning. And it continued to buzz throughout the day as classes passed from here to there, and kids delivered notes and things to various teachers, and the Frito Bandito – our own Scarlet Pimpernel – made his rounds. There was always a good time to be had in the hall.

First-grader David, however, never took part in the fun. In fact, I wasn't even aware of him until we had our contest. He was in the class right across the hall, but even so, I never noticed him, for he didn't speak to me. Nor to anyone else, as I later found out. At the age of six, David was a loner. A dour, unsmiling, don't-bother-me-I'm-busy loner.

We announced the contest via our hall showcase. The challenge was to guess the identity of a one-hundred-year-old item we had placed there – a mystery shrouded in a big paper grocery bag. A descriptive sign read:

> Guess what this is!
>
> It was invented 100 years ago.
>
> We use it almost every day.
>
> What <u>would</u> we do without it?

There followed a list of contest rules: Only one guess to a customer. The first correct answer drawn from the contest box would win the grand prize. Other prizes to be announced.

Marion Hamilton, David's teacher, made a big to-do about the contest, having each of the children in her class make a guess, discussing all the ideas at length, and writing each one on a slip of paper to be dropped in the answer box. Most of the kids were excited by the prospect of winning, she told me. But sober-faced David hung back, fascinated, it seemed, by something or other happening way, way, way down the hall.

"I tried to get him interested," Marion said. "I kept saying, 'Come on, David. Make a good guess.'" She laughed. "Good luck with that. He hardly glanced at the showcase. 'It's a bag,' he said."

"That's right, David," Marion responded. "But what's in the bag?"

"I don't know."

"Well, what should I write down?"

"It's a bag."

'You want me to write that it's a bag?"

"Okay."

"You're sure you want me to write that it's a bag?"

"He rolled his eyes at me," said Marion. "Like a teenager. Then he said, 'It's. a. bag,' like with a period after each word. As if he thought I must be really dumb. He was really kind of funny."

Marion wasn't the only one who thought our contest was a big deal. Other teachers, including those from upstairs, treated it as a field trip opportunity, leading their charges to view whatever the bag contained as a historical artifact and having them discuss its possibilities in relation to the events of the previous century.

Less scholarly in their approach, other kids sneaked in before the morning bell or hung around after school to study the display from as many angles as they could without actually breaking the showcase's glass door. Even the faculty discussed it over coffee, hazarding guesses that were supposed to elicit telling contradictions from me. One of the sixth-graders from the "gifted-and-talented" class showed up with a tape measure to check out the bag's height and width – not an easy thing to do, given that the thing was behind a locked glass door.

The older kids made comments or asked each other pertinent questions: Did grand prize mean money? What did the underlining of 'would' mean exactly?

"That's a clue," I overheard someone say. "Whatever it is, it's made out of wood."

"Ya think?"

"Sure. They used to make a lot of stuff out of wood in the olden days."

The speaker's voice sounded familiar. Could she be the school spelling-bee champ, who had won with the word "gerrymander" in last year's contest? I was about to comment on the little exchange later in the faculty room, but then, one of the teachers made a similar guess based upon the underlined word. I bit my tongue, figuring that he, for one, "wooden" get the joke.

Oddly enough, no one badgered my class for the answer nor even for clues. Everyone seemed to assume that they didn't know anything about it – that they were entering their answers just like everyone else. This, of course, was a source of great delight to the children; they had a secret that even the big kids didn't know.

Guess what! David was right. The mystery item was the bag itself – a flat-bottomed paper bag of the kind invented for use in grocery stores. And lo and behold, David's was the first correct answer to be drawn from the box. Graciously, he refrained from thumbing his nose at his teacher, who had questioned his analysis of the situation. In fact, according to Marion, he displayed little interest of any kind when we announced his name over the office loudspeaker.

"Aren't you smart! You knew it was a bag," Marion said to him by way of congratulations.

"It was a bag," David affirmed with a curt nod.

"He was really kind of funny," Marion told me.

There were five other winners, besides David – a brother and sister team, a kindergartener whose Mom must have read the same trivia column that I did, a "gifted-and-talented" guy (not the tape measure person nor the spelling-bee champ), and someone who called himself Bob Sled.

The prizes for the runners-up were small replicas of the real thing – lunch bags – presented, with tumultuous applause, by my second-graders. Packets of M&Ms tucked into the bags sweetened the deal. Bob Sled – who turned out to be one of the sixth-grade teachers – got special attention. To buck up a guy, who seemed "to be going downhill lately," we awarded him a crumpled-up replica of the "famous lunch bag of Notre Dame."

"Gosh," said Bob Sled when he stopped by to pick up his prize. "Does this mean you kids think I'm a swinger?"

Some of my kids had to have the remark explained to them, but that was okay. They were hobnobbing with the upper classes – something to crow about even if you didn't get all the jokes.

In fact, everyone involved seemed delighted by the proceedings, except for David. He was somber as he accepted his award – the requisite lunch bag and a children's book of riddles.

"I asked him if I could look at his book?" Marion told me later. "But he said, 'No. You didn't win. I did.' He was really kind of funny."

It didn't seem funny to me that the guy who had the last laugh didn't know how to laugh. If I had been David's fairy godmother, I'd have waved my wand and granted him a smidgeon of imagination and a funny bone or two.

But maybe that's just a prejudice of mine. It takes all kinds to make a world, as the saying goes. David was a different kind; that's all.

Still, I'd have liked to help him spread his wings a little. I'd have liked to hear him laugh at some of the wrong guesses the other kids made. It would have been fun if he memorized a few of the riddles in his book and tried to stump the rest of us.

But that's just me imposing my own values on another person. For heaven's sake, I grew up in a neighborhood where most of the Dads and some of the Moms were chemists and chemical engineers. I should know from that experience that people can be just ... different. Not wrong. Just different. Just kind of funny, as you might say.

And think about it: Here was a guy who called it the way he saw it; who stuck to his guns when his idea was challenged; who took himself seriously – really, really seriously. What did he care if other people thought he was kind of funny?

No two ways about it: without any help from me or anyone else, a successful future for David was assured. In the bag, so to speak. Maybe not a bright, shining future. Bright and shining never seemed to be David's thing. But a future in which he might at least occasionally be able to say: "You didn't win. I did!"

I have never let schooling interfere
with my education.

~Mark Twain

At the end of the day, the most overwhelming
key to a child's success is the
positive influence of his parents.

~Joan D. Hall, Educator/Politician

My Mom thinks you're crazy.

~Amanda, second grade

RIDDLE ME THIS

Quite a few kids got our second riddle right. Can you do the same?

Our land, in 1940,
teetered on the brink of war,
And everyone was scared
of what the future held in store.
"What can we do?" the people cried.
"Where can we turn for aid?"
And as the year wore on, they all
were more and more afraid.
"We need a source of energy
to help us in the fray.
"A brand new concept in defense
must now come into play."
But though they thought and thought and thought
and tried out that and this,
They couldn't find a thing that
guaranteed it wouldn't miss,
Some power, some surge of mighty force
that could be counted on,
A thing the nation's fervent hopes

could all be mounted on.
And then, just like a miracle,
the answer came from Mars
In small convenient sizes,
not in ingots, not in bars,
Not in atomic rockets (although
now they are the rule),
No danger of a melt-down,
just a clean, efficient fuel.
We cherish this invention for
we find it comes in handy.
Now that the war is over, it goes
right on being dandy.
And to this day, America
has been a favored land,
For each and every one of us
can hold right in one hand,
This mighty, magic miracle
that made our nation greater,
Thanks to that marvelous mind from Mars,
who was its first creator.
You'll find the answer to this riddle on the last page of this book.

LAZARUS

I call him Lazarus, not entirely to disguise his identity, although that is a factor. The name Lazarus is a biblical reference – an indication of how I feel about what happened that summer. Lazarus's life changed dramatically, and so, in a way, did mine.

Lazarus was poor, had few opportunities, and seldom had been anywhere beyond the few blocks between his home and school. His mother was semi-invalid, having been injured in an automobile accident. She didn't get out much, and she fretted about letting Lazarus go off on his own for fear that he, too, would suffer some sort of injury or … well… she didn't seem to know exactly what she was fearful of. It was just better if her child stayed close to home; that's all.

But while he was deprived of material things and advantages of any kind, Lazarus was rich in imagination, good humor, intelligence, and charm. Oh, that charm. Lazarus smiled and bantered his way into the heart of everyone who met him.

But he couldn't read; that was the puzzling thing. He was almost eight, repeating first grade. And he still struggled with the easiest stories. If he attempted to read them at all. More often than not, he gracefully backed away from the struggle, making a joke or creating an entertaining distraction.

And he certainly could be distracting. He was forever fidgeting, getting up from his chair to look out the window, dropping his pencil or crayons, yawning, and stretching.

"We have a problem, Lazarus," I told him. "I know you can't help moving around that way. But when you do, everyone looks at you instead of at me. How can I teach when you keep doing that?"

"I'll sit in the back," said Lazarus without missing a beat. And he promptly did so. I had to admit that he had solved that problem. Problems were no problem to him. Broken sneaker laces? Use a piece of string. Couldn't find his jacket? Keep warm by running fast. Ah, but the reading thing. He dismissed it with a careless shrug, as if there wasn't anything he could do about it.

And maybe there wasn't. There was a lot of talk about 'organicity' in those days, which meant minor forms of brain damage that caused dyslexia. There were reports that Lazarus had gotten into a scuffle at the age of four. He had tried to protect his sister from a neighborhood bully and was struck on the head with a brick for his trouble. No diagnosis had been made. There wasn't even any kind of official report of the incident — just fragments of neighborhood talk.

"Don't get too discouraged if he just can't do it," a reading specialist advised me. "Not everyone needs to read, you know. Lots of people lead productive lives even though they can't even read the newspaper."

The remark was meant to console me. But it was hard to accept the notion that such an articulate, clever little boy should be unable to read at least haltingly.

Fortunately, there was one more straw to grasp at. Buffalo State College, in cooperation with the Niagara Falls school system, offered a summertime workshop in reading instruction. Called the "language experience approach," it was designed to help kids whose reading problems arose from the fact that they lacked the experiential background to make reading materials meaningful. For the summer program, each participating teacher was to choose a child who needed remedial help, offer him or her real-life experiences, and use those experiences as a basis for writing-to-reading lessons. I chose Lazarus.

Lazarus loved the experience aspect of the program. The simplest excursion to a nearby playground was fun and exciting for a child who had never been taken anywhere to speak of.

Dictating stories was okay, too. But read? Nuh-uh. He flatly refused to even look at the printed words — not in a belligerent way, but with an amused smile and a shake of his head that said more eloquently than word could do. "You should know by now that I don't do that stuff." I urged, encouraged, and cajoled until I began to see the anxiety that lay behind that charming smile.

Finally, I gave up. If he couldn't read, he couldn't. It wasn't fair to ruin the summer fun he'd been promised by insisting. So we continued, but just with the fun stuff – excursions here, there, and everywhere with some of the other kids and teachers in the program. True to form, Lazarus charmed everyone we met with his droll observations and his good-natured complaints about the cost of things. Everything was new to him; everything evoked a comment: – the sight of tourists from the vantage point of an observation deck high above Niagara Falls (Hello-o-o, little tiny people!); the sensation of riding on an elevator (Okay, stomach, here we go!); the challenge of ordering in a restaurant (Whatever you got with a cherry on top.)

Coming from him, even standard remarks sounded like original observations. "Ma'am, I think you made a mistake," he told the ticket seller at a park tram ride. "I gave you $2.00 for me and my teacher. And you only gave me thirty cents back."

"That's right," she said, and gently corrected his math. "Tickets cost eighty-five cents each. Two tickets comes to $1.70."

Lazarus was amazed. "You know something? Every time you go out of the house, it costs you money."

As the days went on, the other kids began to look to him for leadership. Even the teachers wondered about his effect on the people we met. "What is it about that little boy!" one of them said, shaking her head in wonder as once again a stranger ignored the other kids but patted Lazarus's head as he passed by.

Back at school, where there was no one to pat his head, Lazarus dutifully dictated a follow-up story about each of our adventures. Then, he gazed out the window as I read it back to him. Neither of us pretended for one minute that he was actually going to read.

On the last day of the program, I gave Lazarus a book as a parting gift. He flipped through the pages as I completed some paperwork. Then, engaged by the colorful illustrations, he began to read. Really read. Surprised, I put my pen down and sat back to listen.

Lazarus continued for three or four sentences and stopped, his eyes wide. "How come I can do this? We've just been fooling around all summer."

He was silent for a long time. Then, his voice thick with emotion, he said, "Thank you for my book. Thank you for the summer."

Lazarus was again silent as we walked out to my car for the short ride home. Quiet as he buckled his seatbelt and gazed out the window, determined that I should not see the tears that crowded the corners of his eyes.

"Well," I murmured, "Home again, home again, jiggety jog."

Still looking off into the distance, he replied, "I wish it said that in my book."

It was such a Lazarus thing to say – an indirect acknowledgment of my quirkiness, of his regret that the summer had come to an end, of his desire to have a souvenir of our time together.

Lazarus and I both changed schools the following year. Two years later, I met his third-grade teacher. "Isn't he a charming little boy?" I said, expecting – hoping – that she'd trot out some Lazarus stories to tell me.

She frowned, puzzled. "I guess so. I can't get his nose out of a book long enough to find out." She seemed surprised that anyone had ever been concerned about him. In fact, her indifference annoyed me just a little. Couldn't she see how special Lazarus was?

To be fair, maybe he wasn't as special as he had seemed to me. Oh, he was special in the way all kids are, but it sounded as if he had lost that ability of his to win hearts wherever he went, whatever he did. Maybe that charm of his had been a defense – a way of deflecting attention away from what he could not do. Maybe he realized that he didn't need to be charming anymore. In any event, it was my good fortune that I experienced that charm of his, and I will keep it in my memory book forever.

I don't know how or why Lazarus learned to read that summer. Maybe our excursions had convinced him that there were interesting things to read about. Maybe my backing off did the trick. Maybe he was just developmentally ready for the task. Maybe there's something to be said for "just fooling around." I suspect it was a combination of things, but in my heart of hearts, I think – I hope – that fooling around had more than a little to do with it.

Eventually, Lazarus and his family moved out of the district. I never saw him again in person. But in memory, I still see him with that little book in his hands, his eyes wide with a combination of awe and something else that I couldn't identify at the time.

Now, I think I know what it was: Hope – the forlorn, fragile hope of someone who has been disappointed again and again. "Hope is a thing with feathers," wrote poet Emily Dickinson. Lazarus's feathered thing had taken to the sky.

Hope is a thing with feathers
That perches in the soul
And sings the song without the words
And never stops at all.
~Emily Dickinson

Look and see which way the wind blows
before you commit yourself.

~Aesop

I have opinions of my own – strong opinions.
But I don't necessarily agree with them.

~George H. W. Bush

I'm not gonna watch the naugeration on TV.
It should have been Hubert Humphrey.

~Cecily, First Grade.

THE MORAL OF THE STORY

"If you want to send a message, try Western Union," a Hollywood producer once famously advised. Which is to say that successful storytelling doesn't have much to do with the moral of the story. Even so, writers – especially those who write for children – seem to focus on the lesson the story will teach:

- The rabbit who wants red wings will learn that successful rabbitness has nothing to do with flying and that wings of any color just get in the way.

- The boy who cries Wolf will learn to stop pestering people, that is, if he's alive, to tell the tale.
- The little engine in The Little Engine That Could will learn that you can do the seemingly impossible if you think you can.

So what? That's what the Hollywood producer would say. And I think he was right. The moral of the story may seem to be an essential part of the structure of narrative, but it's the characters that draw the reader in. Especially if they have charming idiosyncrasies, like the hero of The Three Little Pigs. What a fun, clever little guy he is, with his house-building skills and the tricks up his sleeve, and his sassy backtalk about his chinny-chin-chin. Why, that big bad wolf doesn't have a chance no matter how much he huffs and puffs.

Is there a lesson in the story? If so, it seems a little obscure to me. Maybe something to do with real estate – the necessity of a firm foundation and a working fireplace in addition, of course, to location, location, location.

One of my second-graders saw the story differently. To her mind, "Don't tease wolves" summed up the story's moral. I didn't argue with her, but as I read the story, the wolf is the teaser, not the teas-ee. But that's just me. It wouldn't be the first time the kids and I had differing takeaways from the same episode. Even when the story's moral is clearly stated as in a fable by Aesop.

The fable in question was "The Ant and the Grasshopper," a preachy tale that illustrates the wisdom of working and planning for the future. You know the one: the ant works all summer, storing up food, while the grasshopper seizes the day, only to end up begging for a handout when the summer comes to an end.

I was reading the story with my average group, my happy-go-lucky gang, my social butterflies. They loved to talk but couldn't stick to a topic for more than two minutes at a time.

They loved to read, but only aloud, round-robin style, with everyone else not listening, just waiting for a turn. I wondered what they would make of a story in which one of the characters was so much like their fun-loving selves.

"Who can read the one sentence that tells what time of year it was?" I began.

Five hands went up. "It was summer," said Joe, beating the others to the punch.

"Who can *read* the sentence?" I said again.

Again the waving hands. And so it went until everyone except Daisy had succeeded in reading aloud at least once. And in interrupting or otherwise offering an unsolicited comment more than once.

"Daisy," I said, "Why don't you read the sentence that tells what the grasshopper did after the ant said no to him?"

Daisy looked at her book, but she didn't read. "Is that grasshopper going to die?" she asked.

"Well ..." I didn't know what to say. Grasshoppers do die at the end of summer. But it didn't seem wise or kind to say so in so many words. Not about this particular grasshopper, at any rate. And there was no sense in assuring her that it was just a story. Obviously, to her, there was no 'just' about it.

Daisy looked up from her book. An anxious frown replaced her usual smile. "Because it bothers me," she said.

Somehow, it began to bother me, too. "You could share with the grasshopper," I suggested. "Is that what you would do if you were the ant?

She considered the idea for a moment. Then, she shook her head. "No," she said. "But it bothers me."

The rest of the group left off gazing out the window or flipping pages or fussing with the Velcro on straps on their shoes. Daisy had captured their attention. "Would any of you feed the grasshopper?" I asked.

They pondered the question for a moment. Then, speaking as one, they announced that they certainly would not. It was like the ant said. If you didn't work, you shouldn't expect to eat. It bothered them a little, but not much. That's just the way it was. Their way of saying, "It's the moral of the story."

Suddenly Robbie, who hadn't said anything so far, pounded the table with his fist. "Listen," he said. "I don't care what somebody did last summer. If somebody's hungry, you feed him."

I raised my eyebrows, and Robbie nodded as if to say, "That's right. You heard me."

The other kids nodded, too, to show that they understood. Then, they shrugged, dismissing this contrary idea. Daisy's face cleared. Not that she agreed with Robbie. I was pretty sure she didn't. But he had said something so much more outrageous than she had – so much more in opposition to the moral of the story. And, except for my questioning eyebrows and those dismissive shrugs, no one at all had protested

So ... it was okay to be bothered. It was okay not to be bothered. It was okay to totally contradict the moral of the story. Whatever you thought, it was okay. Not a bad conclusion to draw from a short conversation.

What surprised me about the incident was how the kids apparently related to the story characters. I had seen them as lighthearted little grasshoppers, living in the moment in true carpe diem style. On the other hand, they perceived themselves as industrious, future-oriented ants, ordained to be judgmental – even charitable – by virtue of their adherence to the principles of hard work and responsible living.

When you come down to it, there was a certain amount of justice in both perceptions. Who of us isn't sometimes an ant, sometimes a grasshopper?

Besides, without any fable to support the idea, the kids seemed to have concluded that contrary notions can peacefully co-exist, that every moral of the story has its opposite at another time in another story. 'Plan for the future' worked for the industrious ant side of their natures. 'Seize the day' reflected their innate grasshopper wisdom. Aesop himself could have taken a lesson from this group. To wit: Avoid an always-or-never mentality.

Sage advice. Nevertheless, I was left with a couple of personal, dyed-in-the-wool 'nevers.' For one thing, I would never again regard these particular kids as 'average.' And you can bet your life I'll never tease wolves.

You can never understand one language
until you understand at least two.

~Geoffrey Williams, singer/song writer

Everyone smiles in the same language.

~George Carlin, comedian

Will ya tell me something?

~Lars, first grade, Swedish immigrant

LESLIE QUICK

Her name was Leslie, pronounced with a soft S – Lesslie, not the Z sound you sometimes hear. To the other kids, the name sounded like Nestle, which made them think of Nestle Quik, the chocolate powder that you add to milk. And so they called her Leslie Quick. Leslie didn't mind. In fact, she didn't seem to notice the nickname. Whether you called her Leslie Quick or just plain Leslie or Lezlie as some of the teachers did, she answered pleasantly but indifferently. In some ways, she seemed indifferent to almost everything that went on in our first-grade classroom. It was as if she were just passing through on her way to somewhere else, so it didn't make much difference, one way or the other, what we called her.

Leslie Quick was indeed just passing through. For reasons I can't recall (or perhaps never knew), her home situation was temporary. The family planned to move out of the area as soon as they could resolve some issues related to a new job, a new home, or both. I never had a chance to talk to her parents – that's how busy they were with plans and arrangements. And Leslie Quick herself appeared to have only a vague idea of what was in store for her. I seem to remember that someone dropped her off at school each day. And someone picked her up in the afternoon. Sometimes, a cab came for her. She called it her 'texxi cab,' and she was quite possessive about it.

Leslie Quick was beyond beautiful, with a graceful little build, a glowing complexion, an enchanting smile when she chose to reveal it, and large, dark, expressive eyes, fringed with long lashes that swept her cheeks as a watercolor fan brush sweeps across a landscape. She was always dressed to the nines in appropriate but obviously expensive schoolgirl outfits that seemed to have been designed just for her. Somehow, she made me think of the fair-skinned Calmady Children of the famous painting even though she was a Black child.

The other kids, especially the girls, couldn't help but notice her appearance. "Look at Leslie Quick," they would say in awe. And indeed, Leslie was something to look at, not only for her beauty but for her unconscious air of privilege, her expectation that she would be admired, her dignified aloofness that was both puzzling and charming.

Charming most of the time, but not always. Leslie had the instincts of a diva, and she reminded us of the fact from time to time. Six years old is an anxious age, what with all that's suddenly expected of kids in school and out. As a consequence, most first-graders get upset about things. But not Leslie Quick. She got UPSET ABOUT THINGS!!!!! Oh, how those dark eyes could flash when the situation called for it. But as I say, those situations occurred only now and then. For the most part, Leslie Quick was surprisingly serene for a six-year-old, come what may.

All too soon, the time came for Leslie Quick to leave us. I remember every detail of her appearance as she lined up at the door with the other kids at the end of her last day. She wore a tan tweed overcoat, with an attached cape and a matching tweed hat with a rolled brim, set off by a velvet ribbon. (I could hear the murmurs: Oh, look at Leslie Quick!). She had such a pensive expression on her face that it was impossible to read her feelings. Sad? Excited? Indifferent as usual?

"We're going to miss you, Leslie Quick," I said.

To my dismay, she burst into tears. "No, you won't," she wailed. "Soon as I walk out that door, you'll forget all about me. People don't remember people."

The other kids tried to comfort her. "We won't forget you, Leslie Quick," they assured her. "We'll never forget you."

But Leslie Quick was inconsolable, refusing good-bye hugs, walking away from us forever, with her back straight, her head held high, choking back her uncharacteristic sobs. It occurred to me that I had never before seen anyone who looked so absolutely beautiful, even as she wept and wailed.

I felt as though I had never before seen Leslie Quick – never really known her. She had always seemed so in control, so self-contained even when she launched into one or her dramatic scenes. Now, she revealed a vulnerable side that I didn't know existed. I had never before realized how she must have struggled to deal with the many changes that were taking place in her life. Never considered that her apparent indifference might be a disguise for anxiety, that her dramatic scenes were attempts to belie confusion, that her 'texxie cab' was both a haven and one more aspect of an out-of-control world.

Leslie Quick was right about her classmates. Oh, they talked about her for a day or two. Wondered where she had gone, what she was doing, whether she had new friends. But then, being typical six-year-olds, they forgot all about her in favor of the new kid in the lunchroom who could do magic tricks. His surname name was Martin, and they called him Magic Martin – a riff on Magic Johnson's name, which was on everyone's lips back then. Those kids just loved coming up with nicknames.

But while they soon forgot Leslie Quick, as children do, I never forgot her. How could I? . The memory of her haunted me, filled me with a combination of admiration for the way she had handled her jumble of feelings, and regret that I hadn't looked beyond her aloof smile and moments of high drama to see a frightened little girl. If I could do magic tricks as Magic Martin did, I'd have arranged to have her come back so that I could tell her that I understood. So that I could assure her that everything would be all right. So that I could have another chance to look – really look – at Leslie Quick.

Most people suffer from an excess of not being looked at.

~Author unknown.

Kids don't remember what you told them.
They remember what you are.

~Jim Henson, Puppeteer

There is never enough time to do
all the nothing you want.

~Bill Watterson, creator of *Calvin and Hobbs*

Jiggers, it's the cops.

~*Unknown B Movie actor*

A MODEST PROPOSAL

"I'm showing a movie," said Mike, the first-grade boys' teacher. "You want to come?"

"What's it about?" I asked.

"It's about ten minutes. You coming, or not?"

"Of course, I was coming. It was Friday afternoon – the end of a long, long week. The kids were restless in that special Friday afternoon way that's exhausting for both them and their long-suffering teachers. A movie – an educational movie, of course – was just the ticket. Ten minutes of relative peace, quiet, and murmured conversation for Mike and me. Ten minutes of who-cares-what for the kids.

Okay, okay. We were goofing off. Most people goof off now and then, and teachers, lest you forget, are people with the same goof-off tendencies as the general population. Water cooler time for most people; put-a-reel-on-the-projector time for us professional educators.

Mike's movie turned out to be an oldie – black and white, with a running time of eight minutes, not ten. Its title was "Your Friend, the Policeman."

Really, Mike? In this neighborhood? "Friend" and "Policeman" were oxymoronic around here. The police showed up when there was 'trouble,' and they came, not to be friendly, but to 'see about the trouble.' Little kids didn't get to meet them, nor even to directly observe any details about the nature of 'the trouble' nor of how you would 'see about it.' But they got a general idea from the grapevine, as they say.

Much to my surprise, the kids liked Mike's movie choice. "Your Friend, the Policeman" was an old favorite type of thing, the sort of offering that Officer Stan, the police department's school-public safety liaison person, had shown them several times. Officer Stan was indeed a friend – a nice guy with no known job description. He did his best with limited resources and even less imagination to teach safety rules, respect for the law, and good manners, beginning each of his twice-yearly school visits with a standard greeting, "A good, good morning to youse kids and youse teachers, too." He wore a uniform with a badge, but I don't think the kids ever put two and two together to recognize him as a real policeman, friendly or otherwise.

They did recognize the eight-minute film's genre, however. And they watched it contentedly, sometimes even joining in its repeated refrain: "The policeman is your friend." Things went pretty well for a Friday afternoon.

On the following Monday, in true life-imitating-art fashion, trouble arose in the neighborhood. The police came to see about it at 11:00 AM. And they not only saw about it, but they handled it with skill and aplomb a little after 12:00 noon, just as the kids were spilling out of the lunchroom onto the grassy play area behind the building.

Well! Here were the cops with nothing much to do. And here were the kids, cute and funny as all kids are. An invitation to goof off if ever there was one. Which is exactly what our friends, the policemen did. They joked with the kids. Played tag with them. Answered their questions. Invited them to look at the real squad car, which was idling in the school parking lot. And, best for last, let everyone who wanted one to have a chance to turn on the siren. The neighbors must have thought that there really was trouble to be looked at, what with all the noise that emanated from our little school playground.

The kids couldn't talk about anything but those policemen for the rest of the day. "They really are very friendly people," said Estaline, speaking for everyone.

And so they are. And so are most of us when you give us a chance to see people in the right light. The right light, as I see it, is most likely to shine during downtimes.

Goof-off times. Times when you're not looking for any particular result.

So, here's my modest proposal. Build a little goof-off time into everyone's schedule – school personnel and civil servants alike. Give it a fancy name – like 'interpersonal social enhancement' or 'community outreach endeavors' or 'beyond academic norms' or whatever floats your boat. Simple friendliness can go a long way toward stemming the tide of troubles in the neighborhood. Or so I imagine. Why not give it a try?

As a bonus, such a program might relieve Officer Stan of part of the problem of figuring out what his job is. He could become the expert in goofing off, having had so much experience with it. Or he could use the newfound downtime to talk to the kids in a friendly way about ordinary policeman stuff so they could finally realize that's what he is – a real live policeman. Or a cop if that's what you prefer to say. He might even spend some time brushing up on his standard English. What do youse think?

FRIDAY AFTERNOON

What shall I do with this giggle of girls?
This wiggle, this jiggle, this giggle of girls,
With their teasing and tattling and tossing of curls.
This certainly isn't a fun day.

What shall I do with this babble of boys?
This scrabble, this rabble, this babble of boys,
With their pushing and pulling and punching and noise
All through the rude rough-and-run day.

I'm getting my bags, and I'm starting to pack.
I'm going away from this yackety-yack.
I'm leaving forever! I'm not coming back!
I mean it!

I'll see you on Monday.

The child knows the television is in the next room.
It's tough to hold a child but it's a lovely thing to try to do.

~Roald Dahl, author of *Charley and the Chocolate Factory*

Fairy tales do not tell children that dragons exist.
Children already know that dragons exist.
Fairy tales tell children that dragons can be killed.

~G. K. Chesterton

Oh, that's *good!*

~Molly, first grade, when the ugly
duckling became a swan

A FAIRY TALE BEGINNING

I didn't get to meet the real Jeffrey until the first month of school was almost over. Oh, I was aware of him – aware of the fact that I hadn't gotten off to a good start with him. But I hadn't put my finger on what the trouble was. Nor did I realize that there was another Jeffrey – a hidden Jeffrey – that I hadn't yet encountered.

We teachers get to be pretty good at handling the livewires in our classrooms – the chatterboxes, the mischief-makers, the tattletales, the comedians, even the defiant ones. They put us to the test daily, and most of us enjoy the challenge.

But the thing about Jeffrey was that he wasn't a livewire of any kind. 'Listless' was a pretty good way to describe him. Or 'lackluster.' Or 'lackadaisical.' Or even 'lifeless.' Oh, he had a corner on the L words did Jeffrey.

Except, that is, for 'lively' and 'laugh' and 'lighthearted.' Here it was, October, and I'd never even seen him smile.

How sad, you say. But sadness wasn't the issue. Passivity was. He didn't do anything wrong. He didn't do anything right. He didn't do anything.

I take that back. He shrugged. He was a master of that dismissive gesture. Not out and out rude, but pretty close to the line. Just a delicate little lift of his shoulders before he brushed a lank wisp of hair out of his eyes and looked away. "Good morning, Jeffrey." Shrug. "Jeffrey, your sneakers are untied." Shrug. "Put your things away, Jeffrey. It's time for lunch." Shrug. "It's your turn to paint, Jeffrey. Want to help me set up the easel?" Shrug. Shrug for happy. Shrug for sad. Shrug for who cares! Mostly for who cares!

"Care," I wanted to scream. And that was the whole problem. I didn't want to be one of those people who screamed. Or even wanted to scream. I knew in my heart that the minute I lost patience with Jeffry, he'd ... What? He'd shrug, I suppose. The thought of it made my left eyelid twitch – a sure sign that a seven-year-old was getting the best of me by not doing anything at all.

To top it all off, there was a note in his folder – a penciled scribble on a scrap of paper. "Look out for the mother," it said. Very unprofessional, I suppose, and I should have considered the source. The trouble was that I didn't know the source. Jeffrey had gone to a different school the year before. The note writer – probably his first-grade teacher – was someone I'd never met. How I wished I could talk with her before I met "the mother."

Ah, well. The year had just begun. There was plenty of time to get to know "the mother." Maybe she'd be just lovely. Until I learned otherwise, I'd let that be her L word. Thus, mentally whistling Dixie, I tossed the penciled note into the waste basket.

In October, the PTA held a book fair in the school library. The books on sale were mostly flimsy paperbacks with cartoon-like illustrations — a far cry from the book fairs of yesteryears, when the picture books on display were works of art. But the kids were excited by the idea of shopping for something to read by themselves. A pleasant buzz of conversation pervaded the library as they discussed what they could buy for fifty cents or so.

Suddenly, Jeffrey shouted. "You guys! You guys! Look at this book! This is a great book! Wow! I love this book! Come on, you guys! Look at this great book!"

His cheeks were flushed, his eyes bright with excitement. He waved the great book in the air as if it were a flag, then hugged it, then waved it again. Was this my who cares kid? I couldn't wait to get a look at that book. What was so great about it? Ninja Turtles? Knock-knock jokes? Creatures from the Black Lagoon?"

Guess what! It was *Jack and the Beanstalk,* vividly illustrated in the old-fashioned way that book publishers in the U.K. favor. It could have passed for one of the picture books I treasured when I was a child.

It cost $2.95.

Jeffrey looked at his two quarters and shrugged.

"I have an idea," I said. "If you and I put our money together, we can buy that book for you and another one for our classroom."

Nobody did the math. Nobody figured out that I was the one who was actually buying Jeffrey's book. He gave a nod– almost a shrug – and the deal was done.

Jeffrey went right back to his lackadaisical ways, to shrugging, to pushing that limp lock of hair off his forehead, to doing not much of anything else to speak of. But for me, something had changed. It was as though a magic wand had lifted a spell. Or a curtain had been pulled back, and a mystery explained. Or a wooden puppet had turned into a real boy – an imaginative little boy who longed to believe in magical beanstalks and giants in the sky even as he moved on to grittier fantasies like Ninjas and transforming robots.

No doubt about it, this was a new beginning for Jeffrey and me – all because of a fairy tale. I no longer had to hide any impatience with him. It disappeared on its own, never to return. Now, his little shrugs charmed me. His laziness simply reminded me of the liveliness of his imagination. A fairy tale – his beloved fairy tale – had given me a chance to begin again with Jeffrey. His beanstalk had led beyond the castle in the sky to form a bond between us.

As for "the mother," I never found out what I was supposed to look out for. Like most mothers, she was pretty much aware of her son's strengths and weaknesses but proud of him in any event. In fact, the L word I had selected for her turned out to be a good description.

Perhaps she sensed my positive feelings for Jeffrey and had no need to be defensive. Perhaps this was a new beginning for her as well.

Jeffrey was a far from perfect little boy. He was a follower, not a leader, so he often got into trouble on the playground. And he certainly would never be a scholar. But now, I saw something special in him that I can only explain in one way: he listened to the beat of his own drum, but he hadn't yet learned how to march to it. Someday, he would catch up to his dreams. But he was content to wait, and so was I.

One afternoon in early spring, Jeffrey sat quietly at his desk near the window, seemingly oblivious to the classroom hubbub around him. His lips moved as he ran his finger down the pages of a book about planes and rockets. Later, he would ask if he could take the book home, and I would say 'yes' even though I knew it was too hard for him to read. Now the sun, streamed through the window, making a halo of his blond hair. Languidly, he lifted his hand to brush it back – that old, familiar gesture that was such a part of him. What a beautiful child, I thought. How could I ever have thought otherwise? He caught me watching him, and smiled, briefly. Then, true to form, he gave one of his signature shrugs and looked away. A shrug for happy? I think so. I hope so.

Oh, my little beanstalk boy. You fell in love with a book. And I fell in love with you.

Though she be but little, she is fierce.

~William Shakespeare, *A Midsummer Night's Dream*
(Little girls are strong.)

We have a mouse in are house.
I want to see he, but my Mom don't.

~Jackie, second grade.
(Little girls are brave.)

Cast into the sea.

~Henrietta, first grade,
as she leapt from the jungle gym,
a.k.a. the Santa Maria
(Little girls are adventuresome.)

Boys are the fastest and boys are the smartest.
And that's the exact truth.

~Jimmy, second grade
(Little boys are the *best*.)

DEAR BIG BIRD

I knew it was a secret, this plan of Laura's. She sidled up to me at the end of the day, when the other kids were bustling around, putting stuff away and gathering keepers to take home.

"Will you check my spelling?" she whispered, handing me a rolled-up sheet of paper. "It's for Big Bird and them," she added as if I might not be able to decipher the large, penciled letters on the page.

The 'them' she referred to were Big Bird's Sesame Street pals. Laura's letter had a little message for each of them: *Oscar, the grouch, don't be such a grouch. Cookie Monster, you should share the cookies.* And so on to every character in that brief, admonishing style.

"Oh, Honey," I said. "You don't have to correct anything. Big Bird can read this just the way it is."

She grinned and then glanced uneasily over her shoulder. Why the secrecy, I wondered? But of course, I knew the answer. A letter for Big Bird was such a good idea. All her classmates would want to follow suit, and a number of them were more polished writers than Laura. And then, her simple little note would get lost in the shuffle.

Well, maybe it would. And not because her classmates outshone her. Shea's Theatre would be packed to the rafters for this Sesame Street concert. Hundreds of kids would be there from every school district in Western New York. Our class would be in the balcony, at least two city blocks distance from the stage. Dozens of little letter writers would surely vie for Big Bird's undivided attention. And Big Bird wouldn't be up to giving individual attention anyway. Unless I missed my guess, he wouldn't be interested in anyone but himself at this performance, instead stewing about how uncomfortable his costume had turned out to be and how noisy the audience was. Laura's letter was such a charmer that I knew it wouldn't suffer by comparison to any other if only someone got around to reading it. A pretty big if in the circumstances.

If it were left to me, I never would have chosen "The Sesame Street Gang" for a field trip to the theatre. It's one thing to watch Big Bird and his friends on TV, a medium that's the perfect showcase for their low-key offerings. It's quite another to see them onstage, the details of their appearances a blur because of the lights and the remoteness from the stage. And even what we managed to see would be just masks and costumes anyway. Puppets pretending to be real people makes its own kind of sense on TV. But people pretending to be puppets pretending to be people was beyond my ken. Besides, the sweet, funny voices of the heavily costumed characters would be amplified and distorted by the sound system and all but drowned out by the unrelenting chatter in the audience.

All in all, this was not my idea of an educational – nor even a merely pleasant – experience. Surely, there was something more meaningful available. A Theatre-of-Youth production, for instance. Or a musical – even a grown-up musical – in which the audience could actually see the performers' faces.

But one of the local corporations had purchased the tickets without consulting anyone. And truth be told, the kids were genuinely excited about going to see a show. Any show. So what did I know?

I showed Laura how to put her address at the top of the page, hastily explaining that this was just something you were supposed to do when you wrote a friendly letter. Maybe someone would send her a picture of the cast, I thought, or, at least, a form response of some kind. I hoped she understood that she wouldn't get to actually meet Big Bird and hand-deliver her letter.

"There will be an usher," I told her. "We can ask the usher to make sure Big Bird gets your note."

The performance turned out to be exactly what I had expected. Lots of noise and confusion both on and off the stage. The cast valiantly sang and danced around the enormous platform, urging the audience to join in on familiar numbers from the TV show. And the kids responded with atonal shouts and periodic cheers. My own kids were on the edges of their seats with excitement.

All except Laura. She, too, perched on the edge of her chair, but she was subdued, clutching her precious letter in both hands as if it were in danger of being whisked away from her.

After the show, we found a friendly usher who promised to personally hand the letter to Big Bird. And then, we clambered onto the bus for a noisy, happy ride home. Some of the kids thought it was too bad that the Sesame Street gang hadn't come out to the lobby to say good-by. Laura didn't weigh in on this even though she must have been disappointed not to personally hand her letter to Big Bird. In fact, she was as quiet on the way home as she had been during the performance.

The next day, at my urging, the rest of the kids wrote letters of their own – wildly enthusiastic thank-you letters to the CEO of the company that had treated them to a "real show." *You should of been there, Mr. Reardon. It was so cool.*

Laura must have written a thank-you note, too. But I can't recall what she said in it. As she had guessed, one letter among many tends to get lost in the shuffle. And anyway, as nice as Mr. Reardon might be, he could never match Big Bird for the kind of star power that inspired Laura.

A week or so later, Laura came to school with a little set of concept books featuring the Sesame Street characters. "For Show and Tell," she explained. "Big Bird sent them in the mail."

She said it in a matter-of-fact way as if she had fully expected to hear from Big Bird. She hadn't looked for such a grand gesture, of course. But she knew he'd get in touch. That's just the kind of guy he was. Laura's faith in her Sesame Street hero was rock solid. She made me feel cynical by contrast.

I suspect that the gift came not only from Big Bird, which is to say the young would-be star who played the part, but from the entire company. It was a fairly expensive set of books – too expensive for one Equity minimum actor to afford. I imagined the whole cast in the green room, handing Laura's letter around, reading aloud their own parts of it, talking about how sweet it was, how cute. Someone probably tacked it up on a bulletin board. Someone else must have suggested that they all chip in on a thank-you gift. And what a thoughtful gift it was.

But come to think about it, what a gift Laura had given that cast of players as well. Most likely, the Sesame Street gig was a professional stage debut for most of them. A rather inauspicious one in the general scheme of things.

One in which their costumes wore them instead of the other way around, just as the tail sometimes wags the dog.

The entire audience had loved them. They couldn't have asked for more applause. But how many in that audience had expressed their enthusiasm in so many words? Apparently, very few. Maybe only one.

That one little girl had believed – really, really believed – not so much in their parody of the TV characters they represented, but in them personally. Believed in them as real people with real personalities, real quirks, real emotions. Laura had looked beyond the silly costumes, the raucous voices, the frantic dances. And she had touched their very human hearts.

I hoped she realized that it wasn't because she was the only one to write to them. That it was because she had something special to give them. Herself. Her deepest feelings. Her love. The kind of love that you have no words to say. But you try to say it anyway.

SWAK

(Sealed With A Kiss)

Nothing pleases me as much
As love that I can see and touch—
A note you wrote in your own hand,
With artful illustrations crayoned
In all the margins. And with hope
Tucked inside the envelope.
How kind of you, how sweet, how clever
To choose a stamp that says 'forever.'
For you are my forever friend.
I'll say so in the note *I* send.

People hear with more than their ears.
People see with more than their eyes.

~Mr. Rogers

Shit bitch cookies are the best.

~Darleen, first grade

My yonkel is coming to see us on Friday.

~Amelia, first grade.

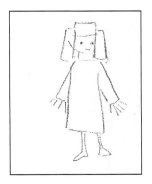

This Catholic girl is going to see her brother.

~Belinda, first grade

BRAVE LITTLE GIRL

"Where is she?"

The woman in the doorway sounded both imperious and amused as her gaze swept the classroom. She gave no clue about the identity of the 'she' in question, but the kids knew. One by one, they stepped to the room's perimeter as if they were part of a big reveal on HGTV. Finally, she – Alison – stood alone, like the farmer in the dell.

The woman clapped her hands in delight. "Jason doesn't talk about anything else," she went on. "It's Alison, Alison, Alison."

Jason grinned, not at all embarrassed that his mother had revealed his crush on Alison to the whole wide world. Just about every guy in the second grade had a crush on Alison. Alison was a star.

Jason's mother looked the object of his affection up and down. A look of mild puzzlement replaced her gleeful smile. "Well, then," she said. "I'll let you go. I can't wait to see the play."

Alison's appeal was indeed puzzling. She was a pretty little thing, but no more so than most second-grade girls. She was neither shy nor particularly outgoing, instead somehow centered in a way that seemed almost adult. She didn't seek attention, but she handled it calmly when it came. She was an unlikely leading lady even for a school play. But that's what she was, and it became clearer day by day that the role suited her to a T.

The play was turning out to be a much bigger deal than I had intended. The script was an adaptation of "Little Red Riding Hood," featuring four or five songs that some of the kids had discovered in an old music book. Being pretty good little readers, they had sounded out the song lyrics for themselves, then followed up by pleading their case for a "real" play in the auditorium that the whole school could come to see.

"We can make up the talking parts," they assured me. And so they could, sitting around the reading circle and offering dialogue for me to write down.

"Now, who would like to read these parts?" I asked, feeling a bit like the little red hen. At that point, much to my surprise, enthusiasm started to peter out. I suspect that my playwrights began to imagine what it would be like to say the words in front of a big audience. What if they weren't loud enough for everyone to hear? What if they forgot? What if they got scared? What if people laughed when it wasn't supposed to be funny? Or didn't laugh when it was funny?

"Maybe I could try," said Alison from her desk at the back of the room.

Sure enough, she could. She needed help with a few of the words, but once she got the dialogue down pat, she took command. I don't know how exactly, but the minute she opened her mouth to speak, she was in charge. Her delivery was steady, confident, convincing. She gave a sense of easy grace even though she didn't move from the spot she'd chosen to stand in. The other kids settled back in their chairs the way you do when you're faced with a foregone conclusion.

And quiet, unassuming little Alison was a foregone conclusion if I've ever seen one. Who'da thunk it?

"Can you sing all by yourself?" I asked her, suddenly seeing new possibilities for our little production.

She took a moment to think about it, then nodded, "I could try."

And with that, quiet little Alison stepped into the limelight, where, it seemed, she belonged. Not that her manner changed in any way. Between rehearsals, she was the same unassuming little girl that we had always known. But on stage – that is, in whatever space we set aside as a stage each day – she became, as one of the songs said, a "brave little girl in a cape of red."

The transformation was subtle, but, at the same time, magical. And the magic spilled over onto the rest of the cast – the village people who handled the expository lines, the animals that cavorted in the deep, dark forest, the gullible grandmother, the noble huntsman, and, of course, the big, bad wolf. Despite a few tumultuous rehearsals during which I pleaded and cajoled and threatened to ring down the curtain forever, there was a very real sense of camaraderie in this little ensemble.

It was June when we opened on our version of Broadway – a time when all the kids are restless, and the teachers are ready to take advantage of any respite offered. Consequently, everyone from kindergarten and up signed on to see the play. The school auditorium was packed with noisy, rambunctious kids, their frenzied teachers, and the few parents who could get away during the workday.

Jason's mom waved to him as we entered, then fluttered her fingers at Alison in a gesture of cozy familiarity. Alison nodded in return, not quite queenly, but pretty darned regal in her own small way.

The play itself couldn't have been more successful. The forest animals' number turned out to be a sort of conga line rather than the choreography we had rehearsed, but the audience loved it anyway. Two kindergartners screamed in terror when the big bad wolf made his entrance down a side aisle – very satisfying. And the noble huntsman, who had worked out a little comedy routine a la the cowardly lion, received a standing ovation for his efforts. Well, more accurately, it would have been a standing ovation, but for the fact that most of the kids were already up, having been on their feet throughout the entire performance, it being June – the annual elementary school silly season – as I've mentioned before.

Suffice it to say, we were a hit – a noisy, chaotic hit – except for the times when Alison sang all by herself. Then, the play remained a hit, but a subdued one that was as startling as the chaos before and after. It didn't appear that she made a special effort to be heard, but a hush fell over the auditorium at the first note of each of her numbers. Her songs floated sweet and clear over the heads of her awed audience and out into the hallway beyond.

By curtain call time, the custodian and other assorted onlookers stood silhouetted in the open doorways, forming a spill-over audience attracted by the music. The effect was just like in the movies, when a young unknown in the stalls rises to lend her voice to the chorus onstage, thus reinforcing the traditional view that talent will triumph if you drop the smallest breadcrumb trail that leads to its discovery.

Alison dropped no breadcrumbs. Nor did she seem particularly affected by the accolades that came her way when our play ended. Oh, she smiled at the grownups who fussed over her. And she was as delighted as anyone when we overheard one of the older kids remark, "Those little kids were good!" But she gave no indication that she was perturbed by the fact that no one in her family had managed to come – no anxious scanning of the crowd, no questioning glances at the silhouettes in the doorways. She seemed as centered on the present moment after the performance as she had when she sang her signature song.

She had a gift, did Alison. But what was it exactly? Courage was part of it, of course. And a certain amount of talent. But there was more to it than that – something more basic that set her apart. Maybe I'm making too much of it, but I think she had what poet Robert Burns called "a good conceit" of herself – which is to say, an unusual degree of self-knowledge.

To make even more of it, I think that quality of Alison's is what is meant by the word 'humility.' It wasn't that she thought little of herself. She just didn't take herself all that seriously. She knew what she had to offer, neither underestimating her abilities nor exaggerating them. To this day, it amazes me to recall how attractive this made her, how it felt like a special grace to be with her, how her courage and daring inspired confidence in others, how it made her seem both familiar and mysterious.

It gives me pause to realize that I never perceived her talent nor the strength of her personality until the first time she uttered those three magic words: "I could try."

THE IMPORTANCE OF BEING EARNEST

If you know the Oscar Wilde play of this title, you will recall that the central character, Jack Montclieff, had an alter ego – a not-so-secret persona named Ernest. Ernest in the city, Jack in the country; that's the entire plot of the play – until it thickens, that is.

My Jack, too, had a dual personality. He didn't seem to do much plotting, thick or thin, instead rising to whatever a specific occasion demanded. When earnestness was appropriate, he was earnest (i.e., Ernest) in ... well, in earnest. But if there was an option to have some fun, he took advantage of it, remaining outwardly earnest but with a knowing twinkle in his eye.

In other words, Jack recognized foolishness when he saw it, and in contrast to most of us, suffered the participating fools gladly. He got a kick out of leading them on, giving them enough rope, so to speak. A case in point, the stranger-danger lady.

The stranger-danger lady had actually persuaded the school board – or perhaps several school boards – to finance a pilot program in teaching kids not to trust strangers. Now, stranger danger is certainly an important issue, and nefarious strangers have many tricks up their sleeves that kids should know about. But this particular stranger-danger lady chose to harp on definitions as if seven- and eight-year-olds didn't even know the meaning of the word 'stranger.'

Jack loved the woman on sight. Loved the opportunity she presented. Asked her all kinds of questions – earnest questions. Was the first to volunteer when she asked who would like to act out a stranger-danger scenario. All well and good. The woman didn't suspect that he, not she, was now in charge. I didn't feel a need to intervene. No harm. No foul.

But then, glancing out the window, Jack spotted someone getting out of a car, "Look, kids," he said, excited but earnest. "I think I see a stranger! I do! There's a stranger, getting out of a car."

"Ooh! A stranger," murmured the other kids, many of whom had wise-apple tendencies of their own.

"Mmm-mm-mmmm!," I murmured sotto voce. Which, loosely translated, means, "Knock it off, Jack."

And Jack's earnest side immediately kicked in, thus heading off an impromptu safari to the window to get a good look at the stranger. Now, that's leadership.

As Christmas approached, Jack trotted out his earnest side more often than not, which was a welcome relief as the rest of the class went haywire, following the education-related customs of the season. He had a Christmas gift for me, and he begged and begged in earnest for me to "open it now. You're going to love it." The other kids caught his enthusiasm as the days went by, and they, too, joined the chorus. On the morning of the last day before the Christmas vacation, I gave in.

"Just this one gift," I warned them. "The rest of them have to wait for the party."

"You're going to just love it," said Jack by way of getting the show on the road.

I did indeed love it. It was a set of "Night before Christmas" tree ornaments – glass discs suspended from tasseled cords, each disc depicting a scene from the poem. A charming gift in itself, but especially meaningful to me, for I had a collection of *Night before Christmas* books that I had shared with the kids early in December. At the moment, they were on display in the school library, eliciting knowing smiles from my kids every time we passed by.

Now, Jack fingered a couple of the gift ornaments, moving them from here to there in the box. "They're not a book," he explained unnecessarily. "But they go with your collection."

The other kids crowded around to see as I lifted each ornament from the box and held it up to the light.

"I found them at the Dollar Store," Jack went on. "I bought them with my own money."

This last detail elicited awed murmurs from his classmates. His own money. Wow!

"I bet they were expensive," someone said knowingly. "They have gold on them."

"Two dollars," said Jack, eliciting yet another murmur of appreciation.

During this scene of holiday cheer, the hallway door opened, and in walked the school principal. She was carrying an official-looking clipboard and wearing a bright smile – her way of saying, "Carry on as though I'm not here." I knew what the clipboard and the smile meant; she was here to conduct my annual evaluation. Ready or not, here I come.

On the day before the Christmas holiday?

Really?

Most of the kids seemed ready to accept the invitation to carry on, for the beginnings of a pre-holiday hubbub ensued. But Jack held up a cautionary hand.

"I have a good idea," he said. "Why don't we read our stories out loud. I'll go first."

Stories? What stories? Apparently, I was the only one to wonder, for the kids obediently settled down at their desks to listen as Jack went first. A few of them picked up the papers they had been 'working' on, prepared, I suppose,' to go second when Jack ran out of steam. Like him, they had accomplished little more all morning than to write their names, but they seemed to have faith in Jack's ability to wing it and their own to follow wherever he led.

Jack held forth for almost ten minutes, keeping his so-called 'story' close to his chest, hidden from the visitor's prying eyes. From time to time, he looked up and said, "Maybe I'd better explain what I meant by that," as though, in reading it aloud, he had just then noticed some logical holes in his masterpiece.

Holes indeed! You could find your way to China through the holes in that story. *Mrs. Pretend-I'm-Not-Here* leaned forward to catch every explanatory word. Clever Jack had her right in the palm of his hand, convinced that both he and his teacher had their noses to the educational grindstone even as old St. Nick was saddling up his reindeer team. I hoped that the twinkle in his eye wouldn't give my own little elf away.

It was then that I realized there was no twinkle in Jack's eye. He was earnest. Totally earnest. Apparently, he thought I was in some kind of danger from *Mrs. Pretend-I'm-Not-Here*, and he was protecting me.

I tried to come up with a way to let him know that he worried needlessly. Those occasional evaluation visits were not much more than a nuisance. A bigger nuisance than usual this time, happening as it had during seasonal chaos. But just a nuisance nonetheless.

As it turned out, I decided not to explain. When the principal left, Jack sat down and folded his hands on his desktop. His face reflected a sense of modest pride in a job well done. Why rob him of the belief that he was a hero?

After I retired from teaching, I gave my collection of *Night before Christmas* books to the public library. I still have the ornaments. They are far too fragile to hang on a tree. But I like to look at them and recall how happy Jack was to give them to me, how proud he was of having purchased them with his own money, how he had topped off this gift with an even more imaginative one.

Merry Christmas, Earnest. Merry Christmas, Jack.

When you come to a house that's two houses
stuck together, the one with the bird on top of the door
is mine.

~Sam, first grade, from a letter to Rudolph.

A NEW DEAL

The phone call came just two weeks before the end of school in June. Her daughter was unhappy with her seat assignment, the caller said. One of the other girls at her table kept pestering her. Would I seat her daughter somewhere else?

Here we go again, I thought. What was it with this class? More specifically, what was it with the girls in this class? At the age of seven-going-on-eight, they had settled into a pecking order, the "in" crowd mercilessly excluding anyone who didn't meet their standards. Which, when you came down to it, meant anyone who didn't live in the school neighborhood, anyone who came to school on the bus, anyone who wasn't a walker. That's what they called themselves – the walkers.

Which, of course, made it a racial thing as the Black kids were the ones who were bused in. There were a few exceptions, but very few. And in our particular class, the only exception was a boy. As a walker, being a boy, and most of all, having no anxieties on the subject, he fit in.

Kalinda was quite another story. She came on the bus, which, of course, excluded her from the walkers' inner circle. Sadly, she wanted acceptance by the neighborhood girls as badly as they wanted to be exclusive. Any effort of mine to ease the situation was met by the 'look,' the subtle way the walkers made their rejection of Kalinda clear. This 'look' wasn't the evil eye exactly, but it bore a resemblance to it.

I had tried to penetrate this secret circle. I talked and talked about being kind, making friends, giving people a chance. I found ways to ensure that kids worked together on art projects, and poetry readings, and such. I partnered them as readers and critics of each other's stories. I read aloud children's biographical pieces about leaders in the civil rights movement, especially the women – Harriet Tubman, Sojourner Truth, and Rosa Parks. I talked and talked and talked. But so far as I could make out, it all fell on deaf ears.

I had never before had a class like this one. In previous years, the kids all got along fine, sitting together in the lunchroom, calling each other on the phone after school, having multi-racial casts in the little plays they produced on their own. They respected each other's opinions, applauded each other's successes, corrected each other's misperceptions. *It's not Martha Luther King; it's*

Martin Luther King. He was a man, a preacher man. Often, the kids seemed totally unaware of differences.

None of this was something I could share with the mother who had phoned. Even though I suspected that race played a part in her child's unhappiness, she hadn't said so, and I was certain she would deny it if I brought it up. Besides, her little girl wasn't really into the snobbish little subtleties that pervaded the rest of the class culture. And to be fair, the little Black child who "pestered" her was indeed a bit of a pest – one of those kids so hungry for attention that they ignore social boundaries and refuse to recognize hints. But she had to sit somewhere, and there were only two weeks of school left. Couldn't the kids at her table just put up with it?

Apparently not. I thanked the mother for her call, and I promised to do something about the seating arrangements in my classroom. And then, I took some time to think of a solution that wouldn't be giving in to bias – even the variety of bias that was so hidden that you could pretend it wasn't there.

The solution presented itself in short order. When I had planned the most recent seating arrangement, my main focus was keeping my rambunctious boys separated. Boy-girl-boy-girl was my strategy. It's one that makes for interesting dinner parties. It would surely work in a classroom as well.

Now, I retreated from that strategy, inviting the two boys at my problem table to go and join their friends. They jumped at the chance, asking no questions, perceiving no motives on my part other than end-of-the-school-year good will. As soon as they were settled, I asked Susie if she would mind taking one of their abandoned seats.

Susie was a dependable child, more serious than most kids, conscientious and rule-abiding, but not a tattletale. I didn't expect miracles from her, but I knew she wouldn't add any fuel to an ongoing fire.

"I'll be glad to," said Susie, responding to my request in her usual polite manner. She gave me a look. Not 'the look,' but a look of her own. A look that reminded me that she had never been a part of the raised eyebrows and head shakes of her classmates even though she was, like them, a walker. It didn't exactly give me hope, that look of hers, but it made me curious as to what she had inferred from a simple seating arrangement. Maybe my words hadn't fallen on deaf ears after all. I could only hope.

The next day, to my surprise, quiet, dependable Susie brought a deck of cards to school. A well-worn deck of cards that looked as though they had seen a lifetime of games of War and Rummy and Old Maid. She showed the cards to her two tablemates, who responded with curious looks and surreptitious glances at me. I looked away. As long as there wasn't any money on the table, who was I to put the kibosh on a friendly game or two? It seemed that Susie was being a bit optimistic in expecting peace on earth to be in the cards, but why not give it a chance?

Guess what! Peace *was* in the cards. After several days of studiously guarding my gaze, I glanced at the card players' table. Susie was dealing. And the other two – the little complainer and the relentless pest had their heads together – not just figuratively, but literally, the wispy blonde hair of one looking like spun gold against the curly darkness of the other. They looked like one of those sentimental Brotherhood Week posters as they giggled over some secret or other.

I had a variety of thoughts and feelings as I watched the three of them. Surprise that Susie had handled things so easily. Regret that I hadn't suggested to Kalinda that she look around for someone more open to her overtures of friendship – someone like Susie. And a sense of shame that I was learning an important life lesson from a not-quite-eight-year-old.

To wit: When talk has clearly failed, shut up and deal.

Won't you be my neighbor?

~Mr. Rogers

Emma felt that she could not show greater kindness than in listening.

~Jane Austen

People love to talk, but they hate to listen.

~Alice Duer Miller, feminist poet, writer, and screenwriter

Come in. Come in. Mike is telling us a wunnaful story about a musician.

Jacob, first grade, recommending his friend's story about a giant who carried a staff.

A SONG, A DANCE, AND A TRIBUTE

Hay foot! Straw foot! Here's the lowdown
On our swinging gym-class hoedown.

In the beginning, we took things pretty seriously at Beech Avenue Elementary- The school was brand new – the pride and joy of the neighborhood. We were all thrilled to be there, students, parents, and faculty alike. Later on, it was renamed Henry J. Kalfas Elementary, an honor that Henry richly deserved for his leadership in the community, especially in race relations.

But my fondest memories of Beech Avenue are of that idealistic time when it was all brand new – the school, the faculty, the belief that we were on the threshold of something grand. We even had a school song, soulfully sung by the sixth-grade chorus as though it were a cross between the national anthem and "A Mighty Fortress Is Our God.":

> Our School, Beech Avenue, to thee we sing
>
> At home and far and wide, your praises ring.
>
> Our principal is kind. Good teachers, you will find.
>
> We're ever true to you, Beech Avenue.

In keeping with the prevailing mood, the faculty sang along, hands over hearts, and the whole patriotic nine yards. But too much seriousness can get to be a drag, which is why we all looked for some comic relief. We had hardly settled into our new digs when the men teachers began to toy with the idea of calling their bowling team the "Sons of Beech." They argued that it would put the school on the map, somehow sensing from the get-go that an argument on the subject would ensue.

And so it did. The school principal, famous in song and story for his kindliness, did *not* take kindly to the Sons of Beech initiative. "What are you *thinking*?" he asked. "What kind of message are you trying to send? Don't you know that children are *always* listening?

In short, he put the kibosh on the whole idea before you could say Jack Robinson, much less, tee shirt.

And so, the matter was dropped. But the spirit that inspired it remained, manifesting itself in practical jokes and a plethora of wisecracks, most of which went right over the heads of the listening children. If there had been a Sons of Beech song, we would all have sung it with the same fervor we applied to "Our School, Beech Avenue" – hands over hearts and the whole nine yards. Or at least, we would have whistled it, tongue in cheek, all the while wondering: do children really listen to stuff as the kindly principal believed? What a surprise! For in our experience, kids did not listen at all. Ever.

"Listen up," we told them time and again.

"I like good listeners. I do. I do," we sang to the littlest ones.

"Tell them what you're going to tell them. Then tell them. Then tell them what you told them," we admonished one another.

Folk wisdom for teachers. Once in a while, it worked. More often than not, it didn't. Kids had too much other stuff on their minds. Most of the time, they didn't even know they weren't listening.

Well, if you can't lick a problem, have fun with it. That was Ben, the gym teacher's philosophy. "You gotta laugh," he said. "You really gotta laugh." His mantra was often accompanied by a wink and a nod, as though laughter were similar to risqué tee shirts – something to be kept from the kids.

Ben showed up at my door one morning, looking purposeful. Instead of laughing, he frowned as he swept the classroom with his eyes. He waved his index finger back and forth, apparently counting heads, then nodded and wrote something in a notebook.

"Let me borrow your class a couple of times," he said. "Just for my square dance unit."

I must have looked surprised or unwilling or something, for he made a time-out gesture with his hands as if to forestall any objections I might have. "Just the kids," he assured me. "You can take a break. Okay? Sounds good."

Having convinced himself that he had come up with a plan that both of us approved of, he bustled off, leaving me to wonder what I had just agreed to. As it turned out, the idea was for my kids to be dancing partners for his sixth-graders. The older kids liked square dancing well enough, but they were at an age when they didn't want anything to do with the opposite sex. Not in front of their friends anyway. My little kids were partners who wouldn't invite teasing on the playground or embarrassing notes written on the sidewalk. Instead, each big kid would be paired with a little one, and all romantic insinuations would be avoided. The end result was that the class looked a little like a Mutt and Jeff convention, and it was tempting to stick around and see how it all worked out. But I didn't. Grateful for the opportunity, I took breaks during Ben's next few gym classes.

After a couple of dancing lessons, however, Ben reversed himself on the take-a-break idea and suggested that I stick around and watch the kids perform. "Just for laughs. Right?" he said, and he waved an rpm record aloft. "Sounds good."

No question about it. What sounds good to Ben must, ipso facto, sound good to everyone. I was delighted to be there, he told the class. Then abruptly switching gears, "What's the most important thing about square dancing, boys and girls?"

He winked, flipping the record album over so that I could read the title. But I couldn't, not even when he handed it to me so I could look at it more closely.

"It's Greek to me," I murmured.

"Right," said Ben. And he winked again. "Come on, kids. What's the most important thing about square dancing?"

"Listen to the caller," the kids responded as one.

"Listen to the caller, and you can't go wrong," agreed Ben. He popped the record onto a turntable with a flourish. The kids cocked their heads in a great show of listening to the caller.

Guess what. The recording wasn't Greek to me alone. It was Greek to everyone. As I now realized, the album label was written in Greek letters, with a decidedly Greek font. The forthcoming music was Greek as well. At least, I think it was. It had a whiney, mournful tone that might have been from a horn of some kind, but a contrasting bouncy beat that made me think of country western stuff. I don't think there were any lyrics, so I don't know how you could think you were listening to a caller or even to a secret signal in musical Morse code. Maybe the whining sound was a singer. I couldn't be sure.

But the kids had no problem with the music. They tapped their toes for a few minutes as if this were regular toe-tapping music. And then they danced. Oh, how they danced: They honored their partners; they did the do-si-do, the allemande left and right; they went to the middle and took a bow; they swung their partners and their corners, they did a grand grand-right-and-left.

"Will you look at that!" said Ben in amazement. "Will you just look at that!"

I was amazed, too. Every boy in the hybrid ensemble was Mr. Smooth Shoes, oh, so courtly as he bowed from the waist or put a protective arm around his partner. The girls, arms akimbo, fluttered imaginary dirndl skirts, pointed their toes, tilted their heads flirtatiously. This was serious business, and they concentrated on giving it their all until the music whined to a halt.

All the kids, big and small, were as pleased as punch with themselves. The older ones even applauded their own performance when it came to an end.

"We listened to the caller," they bragged to Ben. He agreed that they had. What else could he say? That the joke was on him? Of course, it was, but to say so would be to admit that there was a joke in the first place. The kids were clearly unaware of it.

But why were they so unaware? The incident should have provided an "emperor-has-no-clothes" moment for all of them, big and small. Why didn't it happen? It seems to me that the answer to that question lies in whatever definition they applied to the word 'listen.' To the older kids, it meant, "Do as you're told." And that's exactly what they did. The words themselves didn't much matter as long as they knew the speaker's intent. And since most square dances for beginners like them are pretty much alike, they could just politely ignore the caller's speech impediment, if that's what it was, and get on with the task at hand.

There seemed to be an added dimension to the younger kids' definition. Little ones don't so much 'listen' as 'listen *in*. They eavesdrop on the world, trying roles on for size in an ongoing game of 'let's pretend.' That's what they're doing when they play 'house' or 'school,' or 'space rangers' or, as my little girls liked to do, 'fashion show.' In this instance, they pretended to be sixth-graders learning to square dance.

Our kindly school principal was right in saying that; the children are always listening. They are. But not in the way he imagined. They probably would never have actually heard about the Sons of Beech even if the guys had gone ahead with the idea. Our noble Sons of Beech were too discreet for that. But they would sense that there was a joke and that they would be in on it in the long run. Meanwhile, they had examples to follow – to try on for size, as I like to put it.

As to that ban on the Sons of Beech – it happened a long, long time ago. The kids and parents who would have been scandalized at discovering that the teachers had a sense of humor are all past worrying about it. I think everyone would agree that the time has come to honor the sons of Beech, the very devoted staff at the Beech Avenue School: To turn the page, so to speak. So, go ahead and do that.

Listen up, ye would-be sons.
You who were the clever ones
But failed at sticking to your guns –
Your almost claim to fame.

With hearts of gold and language blue,
Couldn't you have followed through?
Then history would honor you,
Revere your noble name.

Was it just a passing whim,
A sojourn out upon a limb?'
Is S.O.B. an acronym
Forever out of reach?

Not so. The truth is otherwise
In fact, such ordinary guys
As you are heroes in the eyes
Of all the kids you teach.

It's well known that they love you best
When you give dignity a rest.
And so, you'll be forever blest
And called the Sons of Beech

INCIDENT AT SUGAR HILL

I was late going home from Beech Avenue Elementary School that afternoon – a rush hour if you don't mind a bit of hyperbole. Actually, there would have been very little rush at any time at that corner if not for the inefficient way the streets are laid out, creating a bottleneck at Elm Court, the tiny, one-block gateway to Beech Avenue and its neighboring streets. It would take two – maybe three – traffic light changes before I could inch my way to the corner where Sugar Hill meets Lockport Road – plenty of time for an encounter with the teenagers coming over the hill, on their way home from Gaskill Junior High School. Actually, there were only six of them, but they made as much noise and bluster as any gang from "West Side Story."

Sugar Hill – that's what everyone called the railroad overpass on Hyde Park Boulevard. Once upon a time, the entire roadway was called Sugar Street, harking back to the portage days when carriers lugged sacks of sugar and other goods from the lower Niagara River to the upper Niagara River, and vice versa. Sugar Street as a whole is gone now. Its sweet name lives on in the man-made hill that then separated a relatively affluent neighborhood of white homeowners at its south end from the predominately Black Beech Avenue School neighborhood at its north end, where a big community garden spread out as a sort of welcome mat.

The garden seemed to me to be one of the essential features of that Black neighborhood. It captured my imagination in a way that other landmarks could not. The community center, the Center Court housing project, Mrs. Field's convenience store, the Baptist Church, Sugar Hill – all of them were frequent references in everyday conversation. But for some reason, the garden was not. In fact, my kids never mentioned it.

Nevertheless, my personal touchstone was the garden, particularly how it looked in the early evening, backlit by the setting sun. A picture of tranquility – folks tending their own little spreads of beans and tomatoes, and okra; old geezers leaning on spade handles, shading their eyes against the afternoon light; kids playing tag up and down the rows of corn stalks, making the most of the last few minutes of daylight. I imagined those kids running to wave to the engineer of a passing train, a time-honored kid thing to do. It wasn't likely that they ever did so, the tracks being across the street and down below them, where they couldn't see anyone. Still, it was a part of my mental picture of the place.

It was such a pretty scene, that garden. Somehow, the sight of it at sunset cast a glow over everything else in the neighborhood. The school building's shining newness might symbolize a promising future, but it was the garden that honored history – the hallowed tradition of soil and toil – an enduring value in a time of confusing changes.

Confusing changes. That's putting it mildly. The Supreme Court had recently reversed its ruling about separate but equal schools in favor of racial integration based upon population percentages. There were, of course, other Civil Rights issues as well, but this was the one that almost immediately affected school districts like Niagara Falls. Suddenly, kids who lived spitting distance away from the Beech Avenue School could be found on buses taking them to less modern – and often less welcoming – facilities in other parts of the city. "Those were scary times," a Beech Avenue grad told me recently, summing up her integration experience in a single sentence.

Scary times can affect how people perceive a "West Side Story" type gang pouring over a man-made hill on their way to a battle to right old wrongs and settle old scores. But the thing was, I knew these kids. I had taught a couple of them in first grade at Beech Avenue. If they were on their way to anywhere, I was sure it was simply home.

The light changed again, and I inched forward, at the same time tapping my horn. The kids, who had by now reached the north end of the overpass, looked up. Their startled faces turned to gleeful grins, and they come on the run, whooping and hollering in delight at seeing an old friend from Beech. I rolled down my windows, and they leaned into the car, two or three on each side. One of them jumped up onto the hood of the car so that he could see me, face to face, through the windshield.

I have no idea what we talked about. Not much of anything, probably. Just a lot of *How-you-doin'?* and *Whas-up?* And *Man-oh-man.* As if I were a rock star, and they were groupies, bedazzled by my headliner persona.

After a few moments of this palaver, I glanced at my rearview mirror. The woman in the car behind me was ashen-faced. Her hands clutched at her steering wheel, and her eyes were wide and terrified.

"Kids, kids," I admonished the boys. "You're scaring that lady half to death." I jerked my thumb at the car behind mine, inviting them to take a look.

"Oh, man!" The kids laughed and waved to the scared-to-death lady. She looked as if she might throw up.

The light turned green once again, and I shooed away the kid sitting on the hood so that I could move forward. "Go home," I told them all. "You've scared enough people for one day."

Off they went, pummeling and punching each other as before. Probably feeling pretty good about themselves now that they were just steps from home, where everyone knew them, and where they could entertain their friends with a story about how they had scared a silly lady over by Sugar Hill.

The silly lady, meanwhile, had her own story to tell. Would it be, I wondered, a hair-raising tale about a gang of ruffians who had come 'that close' to attacking her in her car? Or would she admit that she had over-reacted, the times being so scary and all?

The thing is, the times are almost always scary, and we almost always forget that scariness plays both sides of the street. Scared kids gather in groups that may resemble dangerous gangs. Scared grown-ups cower in their cars and homes, lamenting the passage of some golden age, when people were content to stay in their own neighborhoods, to bloom where they were planted, to wave good-naturedly to a world that was passing them by.

I wished I could reassure the lady that there was nothing to fear this time. But of course, I couldn't step out of my car in a traffic jam. Besides, what would I tell her? That I, too, was guilty of dealing with the current goings-on by looking backward. For that's what my beautiful community garden image represented – a return to a golden age that never was.

There isn't any easy cure for fear, I guess. But it helps to remember that it afflicts us all. And that we can always wait for the light to change, signaling us that it's safe to move forward, inch by inch.

We spend the first year of a child's life teaching it to walk and talk, and the rest of its life telling it to sit down and shut up. There's something wrong here.

~Neil deGrasse Tyson, scientist

That's *amazing*!

~Mandy, second grade, *upon discovering that 23+15+11, 15+11+23, and 11+23+15 all add up to 39.*

YEAH, MANN!!!

When the Beech Avenue School was renamed in honor of Henry J. Kalfas, everyone concerned was delighted – students, parents, community leaders, church groups, the teachers' union, the butcher, the baker, the candlestick maker. Everyone.

But such unity is very rare. More often than not, the very mention of a name change raises hackles folks didn't even know they had. By all accounts, any kind of change causes consternation, especially when it comes to schools. All of a sudden, people have a deep attachment to a numbered street name. Fifth Street School? Now, there's a grand old name for you. Thirty-ninth Street? Makes you think of that movie where what's-his-name plays a spy or something. It boils down to if you mess with a school name, you're playing with emotional dynamite.

It takes a lot of diplomacy to counter strong convictions like that. And at 95th Street, where I taught second grade, we had a principal who was up to the challenge. Margaret Russo was a seize-the-day kind of person, with the ability to turn a mountain into your everyday molehill instead of vice versa, as most people manage to do. As soon as she heard that school would have a new name and that it would be a 'her' name (Geraldine J. Mann), not a 'he' name (as in all other school namings since time began), she went to work to make the whole business seem like a gift from heaven, a totally unexpected stroke of good luck.

We spent weeks celebrating that good luck. We published an easy-to-read bio of Miss Mann. We listened to loudspeaker info sessions about where she grew up, her hobbies, why she became an educator, etc., etc. I don't know how Peg Russo kept up the pace, but she did, finding something to say about our new namesake each and every day. A portrait was commissioned, and after a formal unveiling, was hung in the front hall. The beat went on in dozens of Miss Mann-related activities, big and small.

One of the teachers, who collected antiques, found old photographs of a school like the one Miss Mann attended, including a picture of a second-grade classroom with math problems written on the blackboard. ("School was easy then," my kids observed. This was true, and it says something about how school has evolved into less easy and, in many ways, less successful. But that's another story.)

Anyway, the PR campaign for Miss Mann was so effective that my kids began to ask if she was a movie star or something. One of them came up with a joke, which I can't recall except for its punch line: Yeah, Mann. He turned the phrase into his own version of performance art. His right fist raised in a victorious salute as he dramatized each syllable – Yee-ay-ah, Ma-a-an!

The Geraldine J. Mann fervor lasted until shortly after the portrait unveiling. Then, we slowly got back to normal, but with a new name that everyone now took for granted. Mission accomplished. Then, forgotten – almost.

I, for one, didn't forget that Yeah, Mann phrase and the smart-aleck kid who came up with it. It came in handy when, a few years later, the school celebrated its thirtieth year. I had an entire class of smart-alecks that year, and it was probably foolish to try to get them to cooperate in a performance of any kind. But they wanted to be in on the celebration, and so did I. Yeah, Mann. So, we rehearsed what we called a birthday rap – a riff of sorts on an old Phil Harris patter song called "That's What I Like about the South."

Time out for a little truth-telling: The birthday rap is the only excuse for this entire chapter. It was fun to perform. It was a hit with the rest of the school. And it raised my second graders' self-esteem to such an extent that they were as good as gold for the two weeks or so before school closed for the summer.

A Birthday Rap

Let's give a cheer for the blue and the gold.
We'll shout it right out, very loud and bold:
Hooray for a school that's thirty years old
That's what I like about school. Yeah.
That's what I like about school.

Reading & writing & spelling & counting,
Fooling around at the drinking fountain,
Saying, "Hi, Hank," to my friend, Hank Mountain.*
That's what I like about school. Yeah.
That's what I like about school.

Give me some paints; I'm a great creator.
I make a painting, and a little bit later,
Mom hangs it up on the ree-friger-ayter.
That's what I like about school. Yeah.
That's what I like about school.

Take time to read in the school library,
All kinds of stories, some folk, some fairy,
Some kind of funny. Some kind of scary.
That's what I like about school. Yeah.
That's what I like about school.

Put on your sneakers and tie up the laces.
Go to the gym and take your places.
Time for games and for running races.
That's what I like about school. Yeah.
That's what I like about school.

Morning is over, and lunch is ready.
Pick up a tray and hold it steady.
Hamburgers, hot dogs, pizza, spaghetti.
That's what I like about school. Yeah.
That's what I like about school.

One more cheer for the blue and the gold.
We'll shout it out very loud and bold:
Hooray for a school that's thirty years old
That's what I like about school. Yeah, Mann!!.
That's what I like about school.

*Hank Mountain, our school custodian at G.J. Mann, was a born teacher if there ever was one. He was every little girl's boyfriend, every little boy's hero, every older kid's friend and mentor. He was fun – a great kidder. He was patient and kind. He loved kids, and they loved him back. I'm certain that many a graduate of Geraldine J. Mann Elementary School has fond memories of Hank. Yeah, Mann!

We do not remember days. We remember moments.
The richness of life lies in memories we have forgotten.

~Cesare Pavese, novelist/poet

A poem is but a thought,
a mere memory caught at play.

~Robert M. Hensel, poet, song writer,
activist for the handicapped

Don't forget . . .

. . . . .Every teacher, every parent

I forgot . . .

. . . . Every child

ORANGE BALLOONS AND OTHER NECESSITIES

"Miss Furlong, do you remember when I was a baby?" Danny asked one day.

I knew what he was thinking about – the memorable Halloween when someone's Dad filled the classroom with orange balloons while the kids and I were parading in costume around the neighborhood. It was a beautiful afternoon, sunny and pleasantly cool. The principal had led the parade here, there, and everywhere in the interest of using up as much goblin energy and ghostly enthusiasm as possible. We returned to school happily exhausted, ready to regard the sunset of our day – the orange balloons surprise – with subdued admiration and delight.

Little Danny, a toddler at the time, was there with his mother, who had come to help distribute ice cream and cookies. He couldn't get enough of those balloons, kept jumping up to grab one of the strings. Maybe someone gave him a balloon to take home at the end of the day. I don't remember. But he certainly took a memory home and kept it in his mental memory book until he, too, was in second grade and could talk about it with someone else who was there. I'm pretty sure some of those tired but happy, big-kid second graders who were on hand for the first (and last) orange-balloon day treasured the memory as well.

I venture to say that most first- and second-grade kids retain only a few memories of that period of their lives. But those few are as precious as they are vivid – little successes, little surprises, odd moments that make a memorable impression that we can't explain. The thing is, most of us don't need over-the-top memory makers, like orange balloons. Simpler things are readily available

"What I remember is how we laughed," one of my favorite grads said, proving the point. She went on to talk about how eager she was each day to tell her mother about all the funny things that happened in school. How it amazed her Mom that school could be such fun.

The girl who said all this was in one of the earliest classes in my teaching career. I don't remember doing much laughing back then. In fact, I was in a state of mini-panic most of the time. I had expected to take to teaching like a duck to water. I had assumed that I would prove to be one of those born teachers you hear about – the ones that have an instant rapport with kids regardless of abilities or background or any variable you could think of. To my surprise, things didn't turn out that way. Not by a long shot.

But, as I eventually discovered, being a born teacher isn't all it's cracked up to be. No born teacher ever had what I had, for instance – an inner banshee ready to react in all kinds of out-of-proportion ways in times of stress. A frenzied harridan who sent kids scurrying to their seats to hunker down until the storm passed. It didn't happen often, I'm happy to say. It was nothing to be proud of.

Nevertheless, it made me aware of a heartwarming result of such incidents that perfect people never experience – forgiveness. No matter what I or my banshee did, the kids forgave it without rancor, without reservation, without ever revisiting the incident again. Sometimes in words, more often in gestures and attitudes, children offer forgiveness as a gift that makes each tomorrow a brand-new day, a chance to start over.

Once I had a prolonged discussion with some of my kids about those banshee moments of mine. They had come back from the lunchroom complaining about a "lunch lady" who yelled. "She's mean," the kids said repeatedly. "She yells at us all the time."

"So what?" I responded, unwilling to undermine anyone else's authority. "Sometimes, I yell, too."

"Yes, but …" They took a moment to think.

"But what?"

"It's not the same."

"Why isn't it the same? Yelling is yelling."

"No. It's just not the same."

"Of course, it's the same. I'll show you it's the same. I'll yell right now. How about that?"

"Oh, you. You know it's not the same."

"I'll show you what's not the same. Stand back. Cover your ears. I'm about to yell."

"Oh, you. Now, you're just having fun with us."

They were right on both counts. It wasn't the same. And we did have fun together, partly because another clear advantage to being less than perfect is laughter. What is there to laugh about if everything goes oh so smoothly, as they say it does for born teachers? Not much. But in my classroom, hey, it was a laugh a minute. In fact, very early in my first year of teaching, the father of a super-serious first grader was kind enough to write a letter describing a conversation he and his son had about school.

"What's your teacher like?" asked the Dad.

"She laughs a lot," was his reply. I'm almost certain that he frowned as he said it; he was such a little -sober- sides. He was probably trying in vain to figure me out.

Fortunately for me, the father was pleased by the news that his son's teacher had a sense of humor. And my principal was pleased that he was pleased. And I, of course, was pleased that I had found a way to please. I might not be a born teacher, but so what? As far as I knew, none of them was ever accused of having an overactive funny bone, while I, now having the name, needed only to play the game.

That game stood me in good stead over the years. "You're funny," my kids would say. "You do the funniest things." And they would laugh, it being clear that laughter was not only okay but was an important aspect of the classroom culture. Sometimes I wasn't sure whether they meant funny peculiar or funny ha-ha when they made their comments. But either way was okay with me.

What's not okay with me is the no-nonsense-whatever places that schools have become. For some reason, the powers that be seem to have adopted a business model of education, with higher test scores, not personal development, as the goal – the product, so to speak.

To illustrate: Once, when I shared a collection of Christmas books with a kindergarten class, the teacher remarked, "This is the first thing we've done just for fun this year. There's just no time."

??? Really? When looking at picture books is tantamount to goofing off, all is not right with the world. Fun and laughter seem to have been squeezed out of the school experience for all kids, even the littlest ones. Test scores dominate, even determining curriculum in many cases, making it narrower and narrower to fit a mental picture of a steep upward trajectory – a ladder of skills, as it's sometimes called. Maybe it would help if we substituted a different mental picture – a more attractive one, a kindlier one.

Bear with me as I call up an image that might serve the purpose: When I was in the sixth grade at the old

Cayuga Drive School, we had, among an assortment of so-called instructional materials, a ragged, torn geography book full of maps and charts and diagrams. Not very interesting except for one page that had a picture of a terraced farm. The picture was in black and white, but the subject matter seemed vivid in contrast to all the maps with their map keys and tiny printed explanations. I could imagine the green of the trees and the red and gold of the ripening crops. I wanted to be there, enjoying the sunshine, the fresh smell of growing things, the implied invitation to explore the different terrace levels.

That picture has stayed with me, almost as if it were a memory of an actual visit to an actual place – a place where people could easily go from terrace to terrace and back again, a place where they could sample the grapes here, the peaches and plums there. (I know that a single terraced farm doesn't have crops as varied as that, but this is an imaginary visit, so again, bear with me.)

I was thinking that we might substitute a mental picture of a terraced landscape for that of the ladder of skills that everyone talks about. Just as an idea, a way of looking at things. Think about it:

- A ladder is narrow, with upward the only way to go. A terrace is broad with plenty of room to move around and make choices.

- A ladder accommodates one person at a time. A terrace makes allowance for companionships even when rates of progress vary. Sure, you can have several ladders going at once, but that sort of arrangement spreads a teacher pretty thin. And the choice is between helping one child go as high as possible and holding that child back until the rest of the kids catch up.

- A ladder becomes a waiting game. A terrace offers room for many enriching activities that kids can engage in until the other kids catch on. Is this a way of 'holding them back'? I don't think so. For one thing, there's no prize given for getting to the top of that ladder of success today rather than tomorrow. For another, a teacher who must spend a lot of time getting slow learners up to speed will have little time or energy left for the high achievers.

- A ladder is just a ladder. A terrace is a feast for the senses.

Now I'm not suggesting that school systems throw the baby out with the bathwater. Nor that they revise the whole curriculum in one fell swoop. I'm not suggesting that they change *anything* except, perhaps, a way of thinking. What could it hurt?

Terrace or ladder. They're both metaphors for teaching and learning. They both have upward trajectories (I love big words like that). Why not think – just think – about a change? Who knows:? All kinds of opportunities could open up. Maybe you and your kids would enjoy a few more laughs together. A few more memorable moments. Maybe you would even have time for orange balloons.

ACKNOWLEDGMENTS

Heartfelt thanks to Mike Miller for the painstaking care with which he edited this book and advised me on its contents. I wish as well to thank Michele DeLuca for her invaluable advice; Sue Sullivan for her insightful comments as well as her sharp photographer's eye for typos; and the Lewiston Writers' Group for their encouragement and their helpful suggestions

I have a deep respect and appreciation as well for the boys and girls who were the heroes celebrated in this book. You inspired me then, and you continue to do so now, for even if I haven't heard from you directly, I know that you had the wit, the wisdom, and the love that you needed to lead successful lives. You were all so little when we spent time together. It's been a joy to watch you grow, if only from a distance. You probably don't recall a lot about first and second grade, but if all else fails, I hope you remember how we laughed.

ABOUT THE AUTHOR

Mary E. Furlong grew up in Niagara Falls, New York, where she eventually became a teacher in the Niagara Falls Public Schools. In addition to classroom teaching, she worked on curriculum development, particularly in Language Arts. She also served as a "helping teacher" (i.e., a demonstration teacher) in the primary grades and as a language arts coordinator for pre-kindergarten through grade one. Her publications for children include several stories for *Highlights for Children Magazine* and twelve leveled reading books for Zaner-Bloser Educational Publishers. In addition to writing for both children and adults, she enjoys singing with her church choir and with a choral group, drawing and watercolor painting, and anything to do with theatre.

As promised, here is the answer to Riddle Me This for those of you who couldn't figure it out. Quite a number of our school kids 'got it' with ease. No judgments. Just sayin'.

> As part of their basic equipment, American GIs received emergency kits full of the kind of stuff they would need in … well, in an emergency. One of the standard items included was a chocolate bar, not for dessert, but for quick energy. But chocolate melts, making it useless for its intended purpose. The solution to the problem came from the Mars Candy Company, creators of a way of making chocolate "melt in your mouth, not in your hand." M & Ms.

Made in the USA
Middletown, DE
28 February 2023

25559745R10073